CW00926710

NIETZSCHE

The
ESSENTIAL
NIETZSCHE

Edited by
Heinrich Mann

DOVER PUBLICATIONS, INC.
Mineola, New York

Bibliographical Note

This Dover edition, first published in 2006, is an unabridged republication of *The Living Thoughts of Nietzsche,* originally published in 1939 by Longmans, Green, and Co., Inc., New York. Selections are from *The Complete Works of Friedrich Nietzsche* by Dr. Oscar Levy. The frontispiece—a woodcut portrait of Nietzsche—was made by Professor Hans A. Mueller.

International Standard Book Number: 0-486-45117-8

Manufactured in the United States of America
Dover Publications, Inc., 31 East 2nd Street, Mineola, N.Y. 11501

NIETZSCHE

ONLY forty-five years were given Friedrich Nietzsche for the pursuit of his great philosophical work. Born in 1844, the son of a Saxon pastor, he became professor of classical philosophy in Basle, Switzerland, when only twenty-four years old. There he met Richard Wagner, who was to play so fateful a role in his existence. In 1879, because of illness and failing eye-sight, he had to resign his professorship. Living in dire poverty, he wrote feverishly, attacking and exhorting Germany and the Germans, but he found no readers. In 1889 Nietzsche suffered a complete breakdown and in 1900 died in mental darkness. He pointed out that all philosophy before him had erected truth and goodness as the highest human goals: yet, it was his contention that innate in man is "the will to power" only; that there is no instinct for goodness and truth. Therefore, he strove to produce a man "beyond good and evil," a superman, a lord of life and of the earth. Thus, he prepared national socialism—but that which ends it, too.

PRESENTING

NIETZSCHE

His After Fame

One thinker and writer has lived on for fifty years since the conclusion of his work, and nearly forty since his death. As if constantly present, he has occupied the attention of a world less and less interested in the past. One cannot be considered present merely because one's works are still read and historically assimilated. The number of a man's adherents and imitators proves nothing for his work or its fruitfulness. What is the test ? The work of a man who has passed on grows and changes ; he is still finishing it from beyond. It has long since moved from the point where we once found it, when we were young and Nietzsche was alive.

His work is fearful ; it has grown menacing, instead of carrying us away as it did long ago. In those days it seemed to justify us to ourselves. We understood it according to the bent of our minds, including its excesses. Joyfully we trusted the individualist who was so to the limit, the opponent of the state. He would sooner be an anarchist than a submissive citizen of the "Reich." In 1890 and the years following, this was an attitude of personal independence. Thus we prepared for our own accomplishments, and this philosopher was welcome indeed. He placed the proud spirit at the head of the society he demanded — us, of course. *After* us should come king, nobles and warriors, and then nobody for a long stretch. What twenty-year-old need hear that twice ? Self-confidence precedes achievement ; it is generally strained so long as it is untried ; in the course of a life's work it relaxes, to grow more fundamental.

His early readers Nietzsche by no means approved. He did not wish to be occupied with young people. They were not informed of the fact, or overlooked it. Christianity, which caused him such concern, they believed they had vanquished with ease. "Vanquished" was his word. More gaily than he they vanquished Christian morality. What might follow, they had no idea.

His early young readers, who as yet had been spared danger, hardness, and sacrifice, and whose souls were infinitely distant from such trials, never considered the oncoming age of lawlessness and wars. That age as an experience was cloudy to Nietzsche himself, or he would never have conjured it up. He knew the battlefields of the spirit ; fundamentally he recognized no others.

Yet if the thinker does not, his work does contain chaos, along with the urge to set it loose. His work has lived on through its wisdom, its grandeur. A personality as pure and austere as his was essential to let the wrong and horrible part of his doctrine go on growing along with his noble example, after the proponent was dead. Impure souls never succeed greatly, even in wrongdoing.

Great books have a life which the man who writes them can neither measure nor foresee. They know more than he. They themselves produce ; they reach further than he could. They transform men and things in ways that were none of his will, although his unknown depths required it. On some day which he will never see, they become the uncanny opposite of his obvious nature.

It is greatly to be wished that we should find our way back to the man himself. To track down Nietzsche, discover him anew, would really be to read him again with twenty-year-old eyes, while his thought was new and his fame spotless. In those days his fame was just beginning, and so were his readers. Both were perfectly uncomplicated, reader and fame. The one lacked all the premises, the other had not yet produced its consequences. Nor must we ever forget that our insights could grow just in the degree that his work and fame went on growing beyond the grave.

What He Considered Himself

Rightly or wrongly he considered himself unique. Anyone may think that of himself, and will always have his reasons. When he calls himself the first mind of the century, even that may be true. The century had other first minds ; he was neither able nor obliged to know them. Marx, whom he evidently never read, may explain to the other shade in Eternity that a great success on earth can be measured only by the great opposing success.

Nietzsche wanted to be the vanquisher of the nineteenth century ; face to face with his conscience he maintained the post of a thinker between the centuries. The second half of the twentieth, according to him, would at last realize who he had been. That is the very thing which has now become doubtful : the first half prematurely misused him. It will be hard indeed for him to avoid that succeeding interval when posterity takes a rest from an idea and a personality.

He need not on that account fear that he will be forgotten. He had actually the unique daring to question all that had morally preserved and held together the Western world since the collapse of pagan civilization. The stroke of daring is imperishable. Momentarily putting aside the "revaluation" which concerned him, his share is the exploration of the reigning morality.

He knew that breaking the tablets is not enough ; they must be shattered often and laboriously. It were well to set up new ones in their stead. Nietzsche wished to do so. He was not concerned with the need, nor did he see himself obliged to be. According to him, it is not men's need which counts, but the command of the lawgiver. This lawgiver has only to be the strongest. Accordingly the philosopher saw himself as a lawgiver. Cognition, verification, explanation are nothing ; the great success of the thinker would be solely to command. That still leaves the question of being actually the strongest — which according to his concept he really was, but in the long, the very long view. Hence for the time being he called himself a lawgiver only for his own people.

It was not only through weakness or condescension that he contented himself with this. He doubted, and the doubt was a great part of his pride. Lacking the doubt, no one could be the inexorably truthful character Nietzsche felt himself.

Nor could he be so without the contradictions. He rightly held a high opinion of his contradictions.

Actually he wrote in honor of Christianity more than to its dishonor : try measuring the depth instead of the breadth of his writing and observe where his heart dwells. What he propounded as his doctrine was wrung from his contradictions. More, he won it in battle against his own nature. Though he believed he was vanquishing much besides, his conquest of himself was the thing really earnest and genuine.

And he was jealous of its fruits : to no one would he give his dearly-won truths untested. He must test the truths and the men who presumed to adopt them. No man then alive stood up under Nietzsche the judge. His truths survived his scrutiny at last only because together they made up his work : *that* must endure. He himself in his own person would endure clear into Eternity.

Here we have the astounding case of a man's feeling himself immortal. In this he had predecessors, but they believed in God. Personalities of the highest level (of his level, he believed) have always thought supernatural survival necessary if they were to survive even here below. Nietzsche is the first man, and as yet the only one, to demand of Earth alone that she should speak his name forever. The "thinker between the centuries" was assured that he ushered in no mortal age, that he was in command of the entire future remaining to this planet. With that he had reason enough to call himself the last man. The "superman" whom he propounded visited him only as a shade. With incomparable exactness he saw the last thinker, the last man — him before whom lies everything and nothing, at his feet an infinity, and a tomb which never gives up its own. "One may be destroyed by being immortal."

He said also : "I am a destiny," and first of all he
was his own.   Admitting that the burden of destiny
which a man voluntarily bears is a proof of his nobility and immortality, truly Nietzsche would possess
both.   Jesus Christ, whose place he wished to fill, has
actually lasted out a tiny human eternity ; and he
has seldom been so far removed from exit and decline
as he is today.   In the beginning even His survival
was assured chiefly through His suffering – in the
name of mankind, as we should at once reply to every
competitor and successor.   Nietzsche worked for his
cause with the same passion as once the rising God
and Conqueror of the race of man.   Probably Jesus
Christ while yet on earth planned his "great triumph"
less grandly, and expected it less firmly.   One, like
the other, was for the moment only the lawgiver of
his own people.   The question is whom each considered "his own people."

Christ took for His own the humble and the
needy ; Nietzsche, the knowledgeful and the overbearing.   Which way brings us further is an open
question.   "One can win the great triumph only if
one is true to himself," says Nietzsche, but his Adver-
sary and Brother, too, followed that principle.   The
Predecessor had unshakeable faith in another world,
the successor in this world.   Faith in this world is,
if anything, more daring than faith in another.   If
either man was ever tempted to doubt, it certainly
was never the Son of God.   Nevertheless Nietzsche
thought it possible that one day intuition (in its
philosophical sense) would rule this world.   That
and that alone is his distinction and his precedence.
That it is which makes him a magnificent figure,
and sets him beside Christ without blasphemy.   It

would be altogether godlike to make intuition, con- ceived as a state of passion, the mistress of the world. Never has the world been further from it than now. He made the assumption, and saw himself as the chosen one.

To have believed in the reign of intuition becomes heroic if one includes in the belief even what visibly opposes and contradicts it — one's own contradic- tions, first of all. Such a belief survives by the vanquishing of body and soul ; it feeds on self- denials, the greater the better — loss of health, of membership in society, of friendships and sources of human warmth. In loneliness, faith in the power of intuition becomes all-powerful ; it is at last un- limited, a bare peak of ice. There one's belief in men shrinks to the remnant left by a merciless pride. They are not worthy to read us, and in fact they take care not to. Especially they do not deserve to praise us. That he may have and do battle with adversaries, the single lonely figure increases their stature lest they fall short. A man ! is his desire. A man on whom to prove worthily what he con- siders himself to be.

The Restriction

All this would be totally unbearable, for the spec- tator as for the producer of the show. This is not how one lives. But present himself thus, one can. The terrors of this personality are considerably re- lieved because it offers much, and among other things a show. Nietzsche knew himself, and had good reason to say that one must not do so. Still less would he have the world see through him. He took pleasure in disguise, even outwardly. At times he went out frivolously clad. A man harshly disciplined, implacably truthful, a philosopher of power could hardly have been suspected in that gay costume. Here was a man despising both weakness and pity — but affecting the women who hung upon his words by his politeness and solicitude. Later still he publicly kissed a poor nag, and bandaged a wounded cat.

Which did the initiated believe in — his exterior ? his doctrine ? Neither, of course, altogether. More important, he took himself seriously — how could he not take eternity seriously ? But certainly he did not feel himself at every moment the true hero of eternity — only as the actor in the hero's role. At last he spoke of the "buffoon of eternities," meaning the tragic Nietzsche. He was not unbalanced then, any more than he ever had been. He confessed his play-acting when it was almost over, when the time drew near for the actors to unwig and the audience to go home. Not that this raises the least suspicion of him ; on the contrary it shows the truthfulness of the man, which is above any fictive truth with its contradiction.

"I was never made for loneliness," he confessed, four years before he collapsed under it. Nor did he find himself made for enmities. He challenged and withdrew himself because his work demanded it. His work, something which must be thought and created, demanded of him "the pathos of distance" : on his own account he could never have brought himself to it, neither to suffering with people nor to estrangement from them. Now there are few human types whose will to work can make them capable of every sacrifice. Where is the man whose work convinces him that he must indulge in the blisses of creation with the proved knowledge that no bliss can make up for his ruined life ? Such is the artist, obviously, and strictly speaking he alone. The urge to create without thought of one's own happiness is the special privilege of a few artists of the first rank.

Nietzsche felt intuition as a state of passion ; that is the way in which certain artists work — not many even of them. The further he advances, the more his thinking becomes intoxication, release, wings, relief, devotion ; it is a trial of his strength, a plunge into vice. His thinking takes on the character of the act of love, which scarcely reminds us of philosophy. But it is quite like the shaping of a work of art — at any price, true or false. It has no outside validity ; it requires no confirmation from reality. It forces its own truth and reality, defending them against all posterity, however inclined, by sheer power of ability. Ability alone determines the artist and the part of him that is to endure.

A main question of ability is form : look at Nietzsche and his pride in having changed the German language, in having wrung from it such power "to communicate a state, an inner tension of feeling, through symbols, including the tempo of those symbols." If he proves his character of German philosopher, certainly it is not by unreadability. Whom does he rank with himself in linguistic creation ? Heinrich Heine, the poet whose satisfaction was rhythm and plasticity, who answered attacks on his accuracy with, "But it is said so well." It is not given or permitted everyone to admit that.

But as one example among many, let us look at the
conclusion of the section "A Music Without a
Future" in *Nietzsche Contra Wagner*.

"Music," it begins, "is the last to appear of all the
arts which grow in the soil of a given culture, perhaps because it is the most abstract, and consequently
the latest to arrive — in the autumn amid the falling
blossoms of whatever culture it belongs to."

That might be right, and might be wrong. It
does not fit Beethoven. But it fits Wagner who,
with Nietzsche's help, has posthumously received
the character of a conclusion instead of a beginning.
Wagner's age, and none since, "may in fact help
such an art as Wagner's to a sudden burst of glory
without thus assuring it of a future."

If all were possible, that which follows is alone
impossible. "The Germans themselves have no future." In the first place, why only the Germans?
Was the age which took its evening solemnities from
Wagner a German age? Even Wagner is considered not a German event, but a European one —
this precisely since Nietzsche. How, then, is one of
the peoples which together constitute Europe to
have no future? Thought through, the sentence
would mean that Nietzsche philosophized into space
and for nullity.

But the sentence is a final period which cannot be
spared. If it is untrue, it is all the more effective,
for a statement that could not be expected will thus
seem bolder. "The Germans themselves have no
future": in addition the sentence has the brevity
and force to carry the previous statements if they
chanced before to be unproved — to carry them

through by intonation and gesture. Behold the artist !

Interpolation (if not objection) : Montaigne, whom Nietzsche honored and read, also wrote the following about the art of the word : "Fine minds bring no new words to the language, but they enrich the words they use, giving more weight and depth to their meaning and usage, teaching them unaccustomed mobility, but cautiously and ingeniously." ("Les beaux esprits n'apportent point de mots à la langue, mais ils enrichissent les leurs, appesentissent et enfoncent leur signification et leur usage, lui apprennent des mouvements inaccoutumés, mais prudemment et ingénieusement.") This was precisely Nietzsche's way. His new linguistic creations, "getters-of-the-worst-of-the-bargain" (*Schlechtweggekommene*) or "cultural Philistine" (*Bildungsphilister*), are hardly his best ; they are compounds, for which the German language offers unlimited opportunity — a temptation that ought to be more often resisted. He taught "unaccustomed mobility" to the existing store of words, a real merit. We hear German with a sharper ear after reading him.

The same Montaigne knew about 1580 that, "considering the continual change which our language has undergone up to this moment, nobody can hope that its present form will be in use fifty years hence. It flows through our fingers day by day, and in my lifetime has changed by half." ("Selon la variation continuelle qui a suivi notre langue jusqu'à cette heure, qui peut espérer que sa forme présente soit en usage d'ici à cinquante ans ? Il écoule tous les

jours de nos mains et, depuis que je vis, s'est altéré
de moitié.")   But those are the thoughts of a skeptic
who does not hesitate before his own person : he
doubts their very expression and its permanence.
They are therefore no thoughts for Nietzsche.
Changeable language stands for a shifting life :
we do not long remain new ; in any case, we represent but a limited age in time.   Even in the eyes of
the very next age one is but a survivor, making demands from which posterity looks away, and maintaining laws it misunderstands.   No thoughts for
a lawgiver of eternities, and least of all for the immortal artist.

Wagner

In 1868 a young scholar met an old musician, and
surrendered to him.   The reverse was scarcely possible.   The musician had a stupendous work and
world fame, the scholar at most his genius, but that
was yet invisible.   It was obvious at once who must
worship here, and that meant also who must serve.
A man who was called "Master," and who apparently first introduced this title as a German custom
— what would he expect of an unfinished philologist ?   Certainly not knowledge and information,
unless explanations of his own vast work, tending
to add to his importance.   In the year of their first
meeting Wagner received Nietzsche at his home.
This visit at Tribschen near Lucerne was absolutely
the happiest event in the life of the one.   "I had
hunted so long for a man," Nietzsche was to say at
the end of his short existence.
For Wagner, the young man at the moment was

a pleasant acquaintance; who could tell how he might be useful? His talk was fiery, he was never tiresome, he never forgot his distinguished manners. The Master personally and his professional contemporaries could make little of either distinction or manners; those things are interruptions; all the more welcome an admirer as passionate as he was delicate, who never said a disagreeable word about music. Admirers from other fields grow embarrassing sooner or later; apparently here that was not to be feared. He had sounded the depths of the stupendous work as no musician had, which again proved to Wagner that it was total and universal.

Nietzsche consolidated his position as expounder of the work when he wrote his *Birth of Tragedy Out of the Spirit of Music*. Wagner objected at first that there was much too little in it about himself. That was taken care of. The Master read, and could never read his fill. One had to grow old in order to live again, undisputably and faithfully portrayed in the mind of another, beyond all the disappointments of fame.

This old man's enthusiasm for his glorifier goes beyond the bounds of self-interest. He was truly astonished and moved. "For my part I cannot understand how I was permitted to read a thing like that," — these words he sends to Nietzsche, words different from ordinary thanks. A sublime human process, the appearance of a reborn and wholly pure companion touched the old man beyond his accustomed ambition, far from his urge to take people captive. Only this once he did not speak as the propagator of his work when he wrote "Dear friend!" "Dear friend! Never have I read any-

thing finer than your book." That came from a
human being, out of a much-tried heart that was
alone.

Wagner never forgot what had passed. It was
darkened, it was outworn, their paths soon parted.
Later, in an interval, Wagner took the attitude that
in Nietzsche he had at most lost something useful.
But then death gave warning to the Master; the
feeling of his approaching end brought the truth to
light, and Wagner instructed the sister of his lost
friend: "Tell your brother that since he went from
me I have been alone."

A stronger impression at the very first appearance
is unthinkable. If *The Birth of Tragedy* had
brought every conceivable honor to its author,
still the conquest of the man himself to whom he
owed his book would have been greater yet. In
Wagner's opinion these people went before all other
living beings: his wife, who loved him; Nietzsche,
"who knows what I mean"; Lenbach, "who painted
a grippingly real picture of me." The list shows
how right and proper it was that he should relate
those nearest him to himself alone. He could not
do that with his public, which flowed back and
forth; no extra effort would stamp a face upon the
waves.

It is true, of course, that a picture remains as it
was painted; even a woman may seem to be constant — only a spirit does not. The particular spirit
which Wagner would have liked to hold found more
than one reason to leave him. The first reason was
right and proper; it was the necessity of becoming a
master also.

He had believed Wagner was the regenerator of

civilization — or rather he had wished it. Seriously
this was demanding too much of a musician who
writes for the stage. Did ever a thinker choose
music for his ultimate aims ? Or art of any kind ?
We do not ordinarily hope to regenerate all of civilization at one blow. The case of Nietzsche, not
the case of Wagner, is a unique instance. Only the
supremely self-confident artist at the height of his
feeling would be able to say with Wagner : "If you
like, now you have a German art." Merely German, and merely art ! And that was modest beside
Nietzsche's claim, and less eccentric than his expectation.

In reality art lives and dies with its own particular
society, and its prerequisites are of a common nature ; neither its sublimity nor its splendor can deceive us at last about that. For his Bayreuth enter-
prise Wagner needed a rich, secure bourgeoisie.
After the rise of the proletarian masses opera as a
bourgeois luxury would never have occurred to
anyone ; nor would it even after the arrival of the
sound film.

Nietzsche had been too trusting, and could not
forgive it. Extraordinary music, his passion for it,
and the presentiment of his own calling, all these
together had created images in his mind. They
were dark and they were impermanent — the latter
at least he knew before he admitted it. His eyes
were supposed to have been opened during the first
Bayreuth festival performances. The whole mag-
nificence of a creator who for him was the summit
of humanity suddenly became mere theater, and
not good theater at that. Wagner's audience above
all, that bourgeois crowd with its bustling forward-

ness, is supposed to have unmasked the mere show-
man.   Would Nietzsche have preferred an audience
of common people ?   Wagner was much more the
man to open his house to them.

Let no one believe a word of Nietzsche's con-
version.   On the contrary it was Nietzsche's love
for the stormy artist nature and its music which became a regular torment to him, and finally drove him
to resistance.

Four years of dependence were more than enough.
More of his future than this no one who is in a
process of growth gives away to an existing, famous,
and nearly outworn man.

An old and unchangeable man, he later called his
master.   But who, then, had set out to change him,
to the degree that Wagner was to be a new direction,
whose path regenerated Art was to travel ?   Nietzsche had had far greater plans for Wagner than
Wagner for him.   That made his hostility deep, and
kept it awake to the end — as was right for a hate
that was really love and at bottom would always
remain so.   Nietzsche never truly felt any other
music.   Yet his "politeness of the heart" permitted
him certain extravagances, even while outwardly
the friendship yet lasted.   As a provocation he laid
a score of Brahms on Wagner's piano.   It was his
last appearance in that house, and Brahms was nothing to him.

Wagner even found the wordless action gentle-
manly — the very quality he missed in himself.
"That's the sort of thing that profits one in the
world," he cried, as if he himself had not known
perfectly well how to capture the world.   This
was an outburst that betrayed him, and a touching

one. Nietzsche would not be touched. His last meeting with Wagner, at Sorrento in 1876, finally proved to him that for the sake of effect the old man was capable of absolutely anything. Instead of the pagan tales which people would not hear any longer, the Germans should have "something Christian." Thus an artist apparently shows his base impulses, for shame lest his noble ones should be laid bare. Yet Wagner spoke even of those to his friends ; he spoke of *Parsifal* as a Christian-religious experience. "He wore out atheism first, though," added his friend to himself.

Not even the dedication of *Parsifal*, signed "Richard Wagner, Deacon" placated him ; and here a master was begging his forgiveness. His understanding was asked this one last time, by a man finished and completed.

In 1878 Wagner, in his occasional writings, made fun of Nietzsche — a very trifling retribution, no such blow to Nietzsche as the defection of the man "who knows what I mean" had been to Wagner. It was the end of their relations. On Nietzsche's side they had not lasted even this long. To his greatest human experience he gave no more than four years. Lord of the new eternities, he cut his earthly measures short.

His Christianity

His book *Dawn of Day* (*Morgenröte*) contains under the head of "Wishing oneself full-grown antagonists" a justification of Christianity ; no other modern writer can equal or surpass it.

It was probably written first only to France, as

repayment for the spiritual satisfactions which that
one country gave to the thinker Nietzsche, and
which he never had cause to regret. But anyone
who loves the psychology and the skepticism of
illustrious Frenchmen is at the same time forced by
simple honesty to concede that other illustrious
Frenchmen, and often the same ones, have been
Christians. Nietzsche writes : "One cannot but
allow to the French that they have been the most
Christian people on earth — not in that the faith of
the masses has been greater there than elsewhere, but
because the most difficult Christian ideals have there
turned into men, and have not remained mere images, attempts, half-creations." Then follow the
famous examples : Pascal, Fénelon, the Huguenots,
Quietists, Trappists and Port Royal.

This allows us the conclusion that Nietzsche
would not have been against Christianity, would
not have felt justified in conjuring up or impersonat-
ing Antichrist, if the state of things had been everywhere as it was in that one land.

What did Nietzsche demand ?   To be a Christian
only in earnest, but not to spend oneself vainly to
that end.   Whoever no longer believes must say
so.   Peoples that have never produced Christians of
stature finally lose the power even to live decently
according to that confession.   If only they would
say nothing, and would become what they already
are — godless peoples, men without God !   According to him, this presupposes courage.   Himself —
and whom else ? — he calls "We fearless ones."   He
demands of himself that he "think dangerously,"
meaning by that without God, with truth as his
ethics.

But the nineteenth century, meanwhile, had become godless calmly and quietly through its materialistic science ; it did not on that account believe it was thinking "dangerously." Scientists and philosophers then were not in the habit of solemnly denying Christianity, because inwardly they had never really grasped it. It was the Germans who had gone furthest in religious indifference.

Nietzsche's particular distinction lay in hating the lukewarmness undoubtedly more than the faith. He felt it was shameful to pass over a decisive event, Christianity, as if it could be heedlessly blotted out, as if it had never existed. He, a man of depth and passion, despised his contemporary atheists from the bottom of his soul. They knew nothing of realities ; the human instincts by which Jesus Christ had once reached power remained wrapped in darkness until a Nietzsche should appear.

For him it was of utmost importance to restore the original grandeur to the founder of Christianity, while he was laying the foundations for his own. The victory of the Son of Man, according to this thinker, was accomplished by the instincts of the sick and the weak — bad instincts, if we believe him ; but hostile to life though they were, still they subjugated it.

How did that occur ? A "slave revolt in morals" took place. The strong, the grand, the overbearing were its victims. His *Genealogy of Morals* draws a masterly picture of the process. It is a book of high thinking, and scarcely to be impugned ; there could be no more skilful dissection, no crueler unmasking.

Unexplained, if not untouched, is the miracle by

which a victory of weakness could not only survive
two thousand years, but could beget acts, acts of
the spirit incomparably stronger than those of earlier
historical periods.   Another question : since the so-
called weak and sick did conquer, were they really
sick and weak ?   The so-called strong who perished
or re-formed must have lacked some essentials for
preservation.   Nature, which on principle Nietzsche
adhered to, offers examples enough ; but Nietzsche
overlooked them.

Nevertheless, he introduced both Christian morals
and belief in God into the most advanced thinking ;
up to his time, particularly in Germany, they looked
as if they would be lost without a murmur.   He
alone, outside the church, restored the questions of
God and morals to first place.   He brought them
back to generations of young people, whether the
young people followed or opposed him.

Today it is forgotten that moral concepts were
once a mere empty convention, countersigned by
boredom.   Nietzsche made them intensely interest-
ing.   Purposely or not, he made it possible for people to feel moral indignation without prejudice to
intellectual standards.

Indeed, the most intellectual individuals are those
now most violently irritated by the brutality and
perfidy of outward happenings.   The good conscience that allows them to feel so they have from
one individual — Nietzsche.   And it weighs but
lightly in the other scale that for the sake of his
affirmation of life he approved and encouraged the
brutal and perfidious part of mankind.   "At last"
— the expression he used so well — at last he was far

from depreciating morals ; he gave them a higher value.

But in his youth he had also written : "Christianity cannot be simply practised *en passant* or because it happens to be fashionable." And he had "seen God in His glory when he was twelve." One must have felt the bliss of faith and the terrors of vanquishing it, and probably must also have come from the parsonage at Roecken near Leipzig in order to become what he was, and to leave these footprints behind him.

The Revaluation

He even called it "indecent" to be still a Christian now. This is to condemn morally a state of mind which the nature of man obviously keeps reproducing regardless of enlightenment or materialistic science. Such investigators as Pasteur were believers. The physicist Paul Langevin fights publicly for Christian values in the very midst of an age when brutality and perfidy do indeed profess to be pagan — but in fact are naked misery.

Nietzsche unmistakably shared the superstition of the nineteenth century, which astonishingly believed in the absoluteness of science, and expected of it a system of metaphysics. He did say that science only describes, and does not explain ; but what science could not do the philosopher arrogated to himself. He was seldom fortunate in such steps, and once or twice he was positively comic.

His suppositions on black skin-pigment led him to think it might be the "final effect of frequent attacks of rage, cumulative through thousands of

years." His point here was that the more intelligent
races had been frightened pale more often because
of their intelligence, and then had remained so forever. "For the degree of fear is a yardstick of intelligence." The skin-pigment serves him as one
proof among many that thinking was invented by
cowards, and ethics even more. Every ethical law
at once turns into its opposite, if we replace cowards
with heroes.

That is questionable, and does not decide the real
course of human history. But it is the inner command of a thinker for whom the noble and fearless
are synonymous with the truthful. A man is true
in the sense of life only if he accepts it in all its
harshness. His very harshness makes a noble person true, and he need waste no words on it.

Nietzsche says that the nihilism of all religions
of a hereafter runs counter to life, and so especially
does martyrdom, that expedient of the weak to
satisfy their urge for power.

The obvious reply to Nietzsche is that to be hard
against one's own nature is the most exquisite of all
martyrdoms. With neither God nor friends; the
ultimate loneliness; and poverty; and illness — personal renunciation of a world which he defends and
praises in thought alone : truly no one ever made
his own life more of a martyrdom than Nietzsche.
If only the other heroes and real proprietors of this
world could have a faint conception of this remote
heroism which vanquished so much, but itself first
of all !

"It is my pride to have a lineage." And of his
lineage he names Plato, names even Jesus. Richard
Wagner he leaves out — very wrongly, for who had

been the man nearest him in life ?   He suffered from
his devotion to a music whose motive was salvation.

That and that above all is to be felt in his reassess-
ment of moral values.   This regenerator of civilization discarded romanticism, Christianity, pity, longing for salvation, and fleshly along with heavenly
love.   He determined to be and to encourage their
opposites.   To his ascetic conscious self, though not
in his backgrounds, he was fearless and hard, a great
lord of the mind, light and free, "the most independent man in Europe," elevated above his disease,
strong in his will to power, sure of his permanence.
All this on the foundation of his virtues, and first
among them his truthfulness, "one of the newest
virtues."   "Observe that truthfulness occurs neither
among the socratic nor among the Christian virtues."

He deliberately outlines himself, his importance
and his character, as (according to him) Goethe did
also.   But Goethe was a product of natural growth,
not of cerebration ; he might have achieved perfection and yet omitted to be desperately truthful.
Still, the intent to be always thus truthful is not
only heroic, it is lovable.

Nietzsche is at the height of his cultivation (which
gradually became his self) when he lists his virtues.
"The good four : Truthful to ourselves and to anyone else who is our friend ; brave against the enemy ;
generous to the vanquished ; polite always — such
are the four cardinal virtues."

Unfortunately those are not the virtues for men
of might and reckless affirmers of life where its tur-
moil is blackest and its conscience most beclouded.
But we make no reservations which Nietzsche, full
of great-hearted contradictions, has not already fore-

seen. He knew "where the noblest characters mis-calculate."

"Finally you give someone your best, your treasure ; love has nothing more to give. But the receiver does not find it *his* best, and therefore lacks the last, complete gratitude which the giver counts upon." Who is the giver here, and to whom does he give ? If to uncontrolled life, to a hierarchy of supposedly grand and allegedly strong men we freely present their rights, which they will snatch in any case, we commit thankless waste. People of any rank, especially of a questionable one, will frankly lay aside the traditional, inconvenient, merely pretended virtues far rather than take on from the thinker virtues which are his alone. How many people join in his chorus when he begins, "Yes, barbarism we hate ; we all prefer the destruction of man to the retreat of intuition !" ? We see none of that. "We all" — who are they ? For Nietzsche alone civilization was the inalienable, the only thing that matters. In general people have sold it cheaply, preferring to live barbarously rather than sacrifice themselves for the good of human morals.

Affirmation

And he did his share. When it came time for the decision on his "values," he voted for war — expressly for war with many victims. "The many sufferings of all these little men together add up to nothing," he declared. The misery and barbarism of a continent, following upon a butchery to the amount of ten or twenty million souls — a total of nothing. Nietzsche foresaw the beginning of an "age of wars" ; he never formed any conception of it, even the faintest, any more than of the order of men who start wars.

"In the age of universal suffrage," he declared, "that is, where everyone may sit in judgment on everyone else, I am driven to restore an *order of rank*." In his hierarchy, however, the intellectual nobility is at the top ; but the more authentic that class is, the more surely it settles to the bottom, where violence holds tyrannic sway.

Now that the overturn of values has occurred, this seems a simple thing to know. For him it was not simple. Caught up in a peaceful age, and weary of it, he wanted his "strong men," his "grandees" to prove themselves on their own ground. "The next century will bring the battle for world mastery," he announced to his contemporaries, who closed their ears to just that sentence. They were feasting on the most profound peace in modern history. They, like him, lacked the faintest conception of the war we have since put behind us, or of the war which is now dragging out endlessly under the guise of peace. As was right and proper, the philosopher never dreamed of such a misbegotten compound of war and peace. His strong men and grandees are brave by definition ; how could he have seen them as the cowardly extortioners so familiar to us ?

He was dealing with Bismarck's "Empire," and thought even that the end of German civilization ; he never wondered where in the world his kind of strong men and grandees were to come from.

On the other hand certain memories of the beginnings of modern history — mistaken memories — in-

duced him to represent uncertainty of property,
honor and life as conducive to intuition. "Now, by
comparison, we all live in much too great security,"
he says, "to be good judges of human nature. . .
The choice is no longer : learn or perish !"

There is no helping it, that was his opinion. He
would have thought differently if he had remained
longer in this world. He would have found out
that the command "Learn or perish !" would never
have been addressed to him. The real command
is, "Perish with all the rest ! You shall be the first
to perish, the moment we strong men and grandees
fear your insight. We strong men and grandees
fear everything, but insight most of all. Our frights
during thousands of years have whitened our skin
and bleached our hair blond, as you so cleverly suspected." Such would be the language of the strong
men and grandees to their philosopher if they got
hold of him today, which would be the worse for
him.

To admit the worst at once, he recommended to
the surgeon's knife "all those who would cast suspicion upon the worth of life." Emasculation is a
notion of this invalid who was all too little a man.
He would be astonished to see who actually per-
forms it now, and on whom. Those castrated are
by nature and conviction men ; but those who do
it to them are impotent offscourings of body and
soul.

The philosopher demanded marriage under medical supervision. No fear, *they* are hastening it.

He commanded : "From wars we must learn to
bring death close to the interests we fight for ; that
makes us worthy of honor." To mention only one

variety, probably Zaharoff, dealer in arms and death, deserves veneration ; and that variety should have caught the philosopher's eye ; it was obvious enough even in his day. Resolutely he continues : "We must learn to sacrifice *many people* [his italics] and to take our cause seriously enough not to spare mankind." That is being taken care of now. If he required nothing else, there could be no ground for dissatisfaction.

By today he would be complaining — nay more, he would hate and despise the whole growth and fruition of the doom he hatched, and all those who resorted to his authority. One of his punishments would be to know what intelligences are now mentioned in the same breath with his because they, like him, taught violence. The mere neighborhood of a Sorel degrades Nietzsche, to say nothing of what comes after. Worst of all, he ought to see the type which has since been put in control of violence — put there, unfortunately, with his help. He could never hope to eat as much as he would throw up. Gone would be his curiosity for "rigid discipline," for "violence and craft." His "blond beast" would stick in his throat ; for that matter he never really knew anything of its complexion nor of its low-grade physiognomy. Of his "affirmation" he would not reaffirm much. "The increasing reduction of man's size is precisely the force driving one to think of breeding a stronger race" — here even his language failed, as is fitting when the thought is wrong. "Reduction" as a "force" ?

He would not repeat that the "higher species" has only itself, not the guidance and certainly not the welfare of the lower ones as its goal.

He need only have looked at the "higher species" in the age that followed him to be informed on "will, responsibility, self-certainty, ability to set one's goal." All this is at most pretended by handymen, *hommes de main* with no proper authority and no good conscience. Naturally nobody becomes a "Viking" by simple baseness. That aside, a thinker should neither envy nor recommend even the Viking of history ; his existence was senseless, being without usefulness or common interest. Not a furrow remains behind the Viking, any more than behind his keel on the seas. There remains only the question why a conqueror of eternities should pick out for his parables the most trackless of men. . .

His hard ideas carried him to the extermination of man, that a "superman" might take his place ; this constitutes a mundane metaphysics — something which becomes Nietzsche, but him alone. Why then use examples not even taken from the higher levels of humanity ?

The examples a man selects to make play with are the best index of his own approach, whether innate or intended, whether whim or nature. "The free man is immoral," asserts Nietzsche, who was precisely not that. "History treats almost entirely of these bad men, who were later called good." That is not quite so, and Nietzsche might have known it. But, though his spiritual home was much nearer France than Italy, he never once mentioned the King of France, Henri Quatre. He and he alone is the Prince of the Renaissance. He was the immediate pupil and friend of the Montaigne who still set his stamp from afar on the philosopher of power. But King Henry acted according to his nature when he followed Montaigne : "Every action beyond ordinary limits is subject to an evil interpretation, and this because our taste can no more reach what is above it than what is below." ("Toutes actions hors les bornes ordinaires sont subiectes à sinistre interprétation, d'autant que nostre goust n'advient non plus à ce qui est au dessus de luy qu'à ce qui est au dessoubs.") And of the best means to be a prince : "Let him shine for humanity, for truthfulness, for loyalty, for moderation, and above all for justice — rare, unknown and unwanted characteristics. His business depends solely on the good will of peoples, and no other qualities can win their good will as do these, which they find the most useful : Nothing is so popular as goodness." ("Qu'il reluise d'humanité, de vérité, de loyauté, de tempérance, et surtout de justice ; marques rares, incogneues et exilées : c'est la seule volonté des peuples dequoy il peult faire ses affaires, et nulles autres qualitez ne peuvent attirer leur volonté comme celles là, leur estant les plus utiles : *Nihil est tam populare quam bonitas.*")

The last words, concerning goodness, are borrowed from Cicero — ancient wisdom, a pagan concept of power before it became a Christian one. Affirmation of life may have that tone as well, and it is the sign of a mind which is at one with the heart. Nietzsche did violence to his heart ; his "Yes" is shrill. Success is no yardstick ; we must measure a man by his heart and his good will. In Montaigne's words, *l'estimation d'un homme consiste au cœur et en la volonté.*

Simplicity

From French contemporaries he took over the designation of several decades as the *décadence* ; the word's lineage is mediocre. But Nietzsche used it in a wider and deeper meaning than was to be expected. Above all, he recognized decline as a necessary stage in birth and death. "The phenomenon of the *décadence* is just as necessary as any rise and progress in life." He was indignant at the "socialistic systematists" because they "believe there could be conditions, social combinations, under which vice, disease, crime, prostitution, *misery* would cease to grow. . . But that would be condemning life," he interrupts, and goes on to maintain : "A society is not at liberty to remain young. . . Age cannot be abolished by institutions — nor diseases either. Nor vice," he insists, and thus far he is right. Yet institutions do abolish some things, as we now know, and as he refused to foresee. It is possible that arrangements reduce the mass of human misery for only a limited time, and reduce only that part of the misery which is accessible to the arrangements. But the objection to socialistic "institutions" is suspect as soon as we know that the speaker will have none of them under any conditions ; according to him "the many sufferings of these little men add up to nothing."

By "décadence" he understands, above all, pessimism ; yet who draws a blacker picture of man's fate ? As his antagonists he names Schopenhauer, Bismarck and the "Empire" — a shrewd conjoining of elements which knew one another not. Once again Wagner is omitted, his first "opponent," his trainer for every later hate. He did indeed loathe the "Empire" the more, the longer he knew it, and no less than he loathed a pessimistic philosopher or musician — and for absolutely the same reasons.

The "Empire" was arming ; it transformed a nation which had had thinkers into a "heroically-minded hedgehog." It encouraged nationalism. Here nationalism appears in Nietzsche's work — as a disease, we notice. "The sickly estrangement which nationality-madness has produced and still produces among the peoples of Europe" — he calls it "entr'acte politics." Nationalism and "Empire" — we can tell from his undertone what he reproaches them with fundamentally : they make heads dull, turn them furiously gluttonous. Music — romantic, not "real" music — to him betrays the same rottenness : dangerous through gluttony. His diametrical opposite to "décadence" is clear and free thinking. Decline is everything that enslaves the idea, particularly a state which considers itself instead of considering civilization. As other states scarcely exist, Nietzsche decides that "Civilization and the state are enemies."

Here at last is the Nietzsche who once gave the right to and enabled a forgotten young generation to declare its independence, to be free, after which, in the best cases, came new and independent achievements. We must listen more intently to this Nietzsche than to the Nietzsche who speaks otherwise. These are his real experiences, the freedom of thought and its "hard helotry." For the hardness otherwise so much desired becomes abominable the moment an unintellectual force presumes to enslave the idea.

The "Empire" — the "Reich" that he knew — treated him gently enough himself. By means of "institutions," which after all do play a part in our happiness and unhappiness, it delayed him, though without attending to what it was doing. A national intellectual condition which may have been partly the "Empire's" fault long delayed his great fame. The eager candidate for the great fame found this hard to bear. But he was neither persecuted nor forbidden to write, not even against the "Empire." That is something which has since come to flower, as we see and feel in ever more various ways, spiritually, physically, inside and outside the "Empire," which soon will allow nothing more outside.

Young people of today and tomorrow have every reason to return to a "grand seigneur of the mind" who considered Voltaire his peer, and wrote him a dedication. If only his new readers would learn from him the passion of intuition, and would learn nothing else. Nothing else of his was a complete product of experience, unequivocally meant. He was a veteran servant of the word, a warrior and sufferer for the word. His knowledge of suffering was better than of victory.

The question also arises who his master-man of the future really would be. He discussed the worker ; today it would be pure Bolshevism. *"On the Future of the Worker"* — there is no questioning and hesitation. "Workers should learn to feel in soldier fashion. An honorarium, a salary, but no wages ! No relation between pay and production ! But place the individual, *according to his nature*, in a position to *achieve the most* within his power."

Further : "The workers some day must live as

the bourgeoisie do now — but *above them*, outstanding for the smallness of their needs, *a higher caste* — poorer and simpler, that is, but in *possession of the power*." Only the conclusion of the sentence is my italics ; enough that he went through to the conclusion. And this is in *The Will to Power*, his chef d'œuvre, his last word. He honors the workers as himself ; he demands as much of them as he does of the man of intellect : voluntary asceticism. "We are all workers," he confesses with pride.

He had even more right to be proud than he knew. To promise the power to a new caste patterned on the poor and simple Prussian officers of yesteryear was no small thing fifty years ago ; and thirty were to pass before a beginning was made to the realization.

The prerequisite for these great sentences is a human simplicity which a man finally achieves after encountering complications ; he must have suffered them in order at last to achieve the simplicity of genius.

Nietzsche opened up endless new insights and vistas ; he was ingenious, full of contradictions, always truthful. Every one of his intuitions eventually finds its complement in an exact opposite — these do not : his thoughts on workers come at intervals, on a rising plane, but immovably in order.

He begins by representing the "labor question" to the upper classes, which themselves allowed it to come into existence, as a perversion of their instincts. They could have made "Chinese" of the workers, which would even have been "the right thing." Too late is too late. The class that has become a "question," and which furthermore has been given military training, will wring out more and more new rights by force of those already conceded.

Nietzsche's next stopping-place is impatience, indignation in the name of reason and the working class. "The impossible class are the workers, who should emigrate and wander until they have become masters somewhere. Europe ought to relieve herself of a fourth part of her inhabitants." At that time it could even have been done. Since it was not done, and the "impossible class" would not try to assert themselves "somewhere," but here, Nietzsche was the man not only to concede them the whole power, but to charge them with it as a duty. He was the first outside of Socialism to do so. In the same way he was the only man outside the church to see Christianity in its real fulfilment and grandeur.

For he himself felt grandly ; but grandeur, his or any other, compels simplicity. We cannot be grand by simple will-power, even though Nietzsche believed we could. Discipline and "on the other hand" annihilation — that is the mistake of a high mind about itself and its nature.

Greatness shows itself in the severe modesty with which it helps others up, although and because it overtops them. To recognize and pronounce simple truths ; to promise and give men a simple contentment : beyond that the greatest of men can do nothing, or can at most forbear. After all, he orders his "higher caste" : for power's sake, be poor ; remain simple and poor.

That is the last word and the end of this thinker's tragedy, as grievous as it is beautiful. He fought his way out of a world of decay, which he was too

sick — he thought too healthy — to accept. Why
did he love and hate Wagner? Wagner was
equipped to withstand the *décadence*, and even
added its charms to his own great work. Nietzsche
was driven from pillar to post between science and
Christianity, skepticism, faith and superstition, denial and affirmation, great artistic creation, spiritual
pride, and his claim to an unbounded fame ; on top
of all the rest, Nietzsche suffered the agonizing, bliss-
ful fascination of Eternity.

Eternal

A sick man has been known to approve and love
his doom, even to the extent of wishing it might
never end. Nietzsche wished to be immortal, and
that without change, with all his physical pains,
with the spiritual flaws which he was forever mastering, with his loneliness, the hatred that crowded in,
the shadows of friends who never came, of women
who could never give warm illusions to the frozen
man. It was a life bearable only by the arts of his
will, by reinterpretation and supreme effort : he
convinced himself it was good, worthy of repetition,
and not of one only. Amid this mortal coil, where
none of us knows his way, he felt assured of being
eternal on earth. If to none of his other incarna-
tions, we must certainly bow to the Nietzsche who
by force of his acquiescence, *amor fati*, finally became in fact immortal.

At first he was an ordinary invalid, subject to
that failure of the nerves which was a regular plague
in the last third of the century. Medical science
could not keep up ; the most important nervous

center was usually ignored, and there was no therapy
of the sympathetic system.

At the age of twenty-five Nietzsche had received
a call to Basel as a professor.

Ten years later, with Wagner behind him, he cut
loose from his post, from people, particularly from
doctors. By then he had only another ten years for
everything he demanded of himself : an intellectual
edifice, power through that work ; to outshine every
other fame ; to be immortal — and thus be sound in
health.

Out of all his suffering he made a new, higher
health ; he pronounced himself sound. "Sickness
may actually be inner soundness, and vice versa.
Health is something personal : it is what serves a
man and his work, though to others it may mean
disease." He urgently insisted upon it. "I have
not a single sickly trait ; even in times of gravest
sickness I have never been sickly."

The work of a man in health, he believed, must be
easily performed — a mistake ; healthy persons can
never have difficulty enough. He denied that he
exerted himself. He said his profession was easy,
really mere idling. We can guess at once whom
he was always thinking of. A worker who labored
intensely for his great work was Wagner. That
work had not only mass but weight. His portraitist,
Lenbach, said to Wagner : "Your music is a freight
wagon to the Kingdom of Heaven." Consequently
— a consequently that led far, finally into madness —
Nietzsche's antagonist "was not at liberty" to have
inhibitions or to strive and be heavy-laden. Meta-
phorically and literally he must be a dancer, supple-
limbed and quick-thinking. Nietzsche tolerated

only those ideas which had been "conceived while strolling" — he could have said "while climbing."

Dionysus is a tragic god whom Nietzsche transformed until at last life had a dionysian justification, "even at its most fearful, most ambiguous, and most mendacious." The sufferer saw this figure of unmoral joy and lightness as the image of his own nature, "the highest nature of all being." "Through every abyss I still carry my beneficent Yes."

And in view of what he achieved he was right ; he was right to the very brink of madness, which he never foresaw. Just before it, he hoped for a fatal stroke, and thus undeniably exposed a weakness. It was a grave exposure of his "beneficent Yes." He hoped to die quickly.

In the meantime he mastered his thoughts, no matter how dionysically exaggerated they became. Even in *Ecce Homo* they never went off the track. There he wrote of himself as the ecstatic worshiper of an eternal God might talk two thousand years after. Was he not the god ? If a man wants a great work and a great life, he wants it all, including the end. In 1880 he was the only man with the astonishing knowledge of a world crisis to come. In 1888, in a letter for which as a matter of fact his mind was no longer responsible, he wanted "to lash the Empire in an iron shirt, and provoke it to a war of desperation." That was madness only in respect to the date, and a most prophetic madness.

He assumed almost everything from the beginning. Of his great fame he was sure when no one knew him and his few friends were glad of any pretext to fall away from an uncanny figure — uncanny through the very immensity of its future. He flung himself upon every distant sign of fame, and trembled at every delay. "The Germans will try again in my case to bring forth a mouse out of an enormous destiny."

This all begins by presupposing that he believed in fame. But fame is a classic-romantic conception ; modern man has been taught differently. Fame includes vicissitudes, misunderstandings, embalmed masks, and finally ends as an empty name. Fame looks exceedingly like the grave. But Flaubert exclaimed : "To create lasting works, you must not laugh at fame." And Nietzsche took him seriously, took him sacredly. Both of them thought little of mankind, and everything of their standing in its eyes. Presumably not for mankind's sake but for jealousy of their predecessors they felt obliged to join "the busts that survive the city."

Nietzsche saw Wagner, and Wagner only. Of *Parsifal* he thought : "a stroke of genius of seduction." Yet later : "I cannot think of it without being staggered." Anyone who pretended to Nietzsche's own estimate of Wagner was "irreverent riffraff." Then again, "Now I must not even compare myself with him any more ; I belong to a different rank." And at last : "With real horror I discover how nearly related to Wagner I really am." This shortly before his own race was run. And this stands above all : "I loved him, and no one else. He was a man after my own heart."

By supposition fame is earthly immortality. Earthly immortality is no whit less doubtful than any heavenly life. Enough that several latter-day heroes have confidently expected the reward of their high aims and desperate striving ; they demanded to be immortal, here or beyond, preferably both. Nietzsche confined himself to the here — it is not a smaller demand, since he wanted more than merely spiritual survival. He propounded a doctrine which permitted him eternally to return in his own person, but really to stay here from the beginning. For those who are buried, billions of years do not count even as one day. If a man arise again after aeons, from head to foot the same who once appeared to perish, he has never perished. The door through which he departed remains open ; his shadow still moves here within ; and here he is, already on the threshold which he had barely crossed.

That is the concept. Can he possibly not have seen that it is borrowed from the belief in eternal blessedness, and recasts it — recasts it not to advantage ? We imagine the blessed as released from their earthly shortcomings and sufferings. Nietzsche reborn will be the same Nietzsche, suffering and struggling as before, and so many times over. The ability to grow out of his errors is not vouchsafed him, and his infirmities are forever incurable.

The claim that faith saves is in itself a new faith, he has been heard to say. The claim that faith is perdition, compelling us, barely in our coffins, to go through the old, all-too-familiar life again — *that* faith is a different matter ! It is scientifically proved. With pomp and circumstance the science of the nineteenth century comes to its defense. "The doctrine of the conservation of energy demands eternal recurrence." Such is the discovery of the philosopher who carries the nineteenth century on his boot-soles into Eternity.

"The world as a force must not be conceived

as unlimited ; we reject the concept of an infinite
force as irreconcilable with the concept of 'force.'
Therefore the world lacks the potentiality of eternal
newness." A profound humorist named Christian
Morgenstern caught up something similar in a verse :
"That *cannot* be which *may* not be."

The doctrine of the conservation of energy promises the dead at most that a fruit tree shall grow from
their graves. Eternal recurrence ? The unique,
"non-recurrent" Nietzsche was necessary to grasp
and hold it.

He owed it to himself to leave a doctrine behind,
and traditionally that would be a faith. Science
was supposed to be the basis of this faith here ; in
reality, as always, the basis was a person. "I have
tried to deny everything : oh, tearing down is easy,
but building up !" There the root lies open. No
matter how he boasted of his isolated greatness, he
had honest doubts of its fruitfulness. Yet he wanted
to serve, but in his own austere way. "Anyone
who hopes to recover a single experience must wish
them all back." His doctrine "shall be the religion of the freest, gayest, and noblest souls — a
lovely meadow between gilded ice and clear sky !"
He demanded courage, and created his own for an
immortality which does not console, and for a fearful eternity. "Immortal is the instant when I begot
resurrection. For the sake of that instant I will
bear my resurrection."

Requiescat in pace.

Heinrich Mann has selected and arranged
the essence of Nietzsche's thought from

THE BIRTH OF TRAGEDY
THOUGHTS OUT OF SEASON
THE DAWN OF DAY
THE JOYFUL WISDOM
THUS SPAKE ZARATHUSTRA
BEYOND GOOD AND EVIL
THE GENEALOGY OF MORALS
THE CASE OF WAGNER
NIETZSCHE CONTRA WAGNER
THE TWILIGHT OF THE IDOLS
THE ANTICHRIST
ECCE HOMO
THE WILL TO POWER

THE WORKS OF
FRIEDRICH NIETZSCHE
(1844–1900)

The Birth of Tragedy Out of the Spirit of Music
   (1870–1)
Thoughts Out of Season (1873–76)
Human All-Too Human (1878–80)
The Dawn of Day (1881)
The Joyful Wisdom (1883)
Thus Spake Zarathustra (1883–91)
Beyond Good and Evil (1885–86)
The Genealogy of Morals (1887)
The Case of Wagner (1888)
The Antichrist (1888)
Ecce Homo (1888)
The Twilight of the Idols (1889)

I

SCIENCE, PHILOSOPHY, TRUTH

There is a profound and fundamental satisfaction in the fact that science ascertains things that hold their ground, and again furnish the basis for new researches : — it could certainly be otherwise. Indeed, we are so much convinced of all the uncertainty and caprice of our judgments, and of the everlasting change of all human laws and conceptions, that we are really astonished how persistently the results of science hold their ground ! In earlier times people knew nothing of this changeability of all human things ; the custom of morality maintained the belief that the whole inner life of man was bound to iron necessity by eternal fetters : — perhaps people then felt a similar voluptuousness of astonishment when they listened to tales and fairy stories. The wonderful did so much good to those men, who might well get tired sometimes of the regular and the eternal. To leave the ground for once ! To soar ! To stray ! To be mad ! — that belonged to the paradise and the revelry of earlier times ; while our felicity is like that of the shipwrecked man who has gone ashore, and places himself with both feet on the old, firm ground — in astonishment that it does not rock.

You ask me what all idiosyncrasy is in philosophers ? . . . For instance their lack of the historical sense, their hatred even of the idea of Becoming, their Egyptianism. They imagine that they do honour to a thing by divorcing it from history *sub specie æterni*, — when they make a mummy of it. All the ideas that philosophers have treated for thousands of years, have been mummied concepts ; nothing real has ever come out of their hands alive. These idolaters of concepts merely kill and stuff things when they worship, — they threaten the life of everything they adore. Death, change, age, as well as procreation and growth, are in their opinion objections, — even refutations. That which is cannot evolve ; that which evolves *is* not. Now all of them believe, and even with desperation, in Being. But, as they cannot lay hold of it, they try to discover reasons why this privilege is withheld from them. "Some merely apparent quality, some deception must be the cause of our not being able to ascertain the nature of Being : where is the deceiver ?" "We have him," they cry rejoicing, "it is sensuality !" These senses, *which in other things are so immoral*, cheat us concerning the true world. Moral : we must get rid of the deception of the senses, of Becoming, of history, of falsehood. — History is nothing more than the belief in the senses, the belief in falsehood. Moral : we must say "no" to everything in which the senses believe : to all the rest of mankind : all that belongs to the "people." Let us be philosophers, mummies, monotonotheists, grave-diggers ! — And above all, away with the body, this wretched *idée fixe* of the senses, infected with all the faults of logic that exist, refuted, even impossible, although it be impudent enough to pose as if it were real !

With a feeling of great reverence I except the name of *Heraclitus*. If the rest of the philosophic gang rejected the evidences of the senses, because the latter revealed a state of multifariousness and change, he rejected the same evidence because it revealed things as if they possessed permanence and unity. Even Heraclitus did an injustice to the senses. The latter lie neither as the Eleatics believed them to lie, nor as he believed them to lie, — they do not lie at all. The interpretations we give to their evidence is what first introduces falsehood into it ; for instance the lie of unity, the lie of matter, of substance and of permanence. Reason is the cause of our falsifying the evidence of the senses. In so far as the senses show us a state of Becoming, of transiency, and of change, they do not lie. But in declaring that Being was an empty illusion, Heraclitus will remain eternally right. The "apparent" world is the only world : the "true world" is no more than a false adjunct thereto.

And what delicate instruments of observation we have in our senses ! This human nose, for instance, of which no philosopher has yet spoken with reverence and gratitude, is, for the present, the most finely adjusted instrument at our disposal : it is able to register even such slight changes of movement as the spectroscope would be unable to record. Our scientific triumphs at the present day extend precisely so far as we have accepted the evidence of our senses, — as we have sharpened and armed them, and learned to follow them up to the end. What remains is abortive and not yet science — that is to say, metaphysics, theology, psychology, epistemology, or formal science, or a doctrine of symbols, like logic and its applied form mathematics. In all these things reality does not come into consideration at all, even as a problem ; just as little as does the question concerning the general value of such a convention of symbols as logic.

*   *   *

The progress of science is at the present time no longer hindered by the purely accidental fact that man attains to about seventy years, which was the case far too long. In former times people wished to master the entire extent of knowledge within this period, and all the methods of knowledge were valued according to this general desire. Minor questions and individual experiments were looked upon as unworthy of notice : people wanted to take the shortest path under the impression that, since everything in this world seemed to be arranged with a view to man's needs, even the acquirement of knowledge was regulated in view of the limits of human life.

To solve everything at a single stroke, with one word — this was the secret desire ; and the task was represented in the symbol of the Gordian knot or the egg of Columbus. No one doubted that it was possible to reach the goal of knowledge after the manner of Alexander or Columbus, and to settle all questions with one answer. "There is a mystery to be solved," seemed to be the aim of life in the eyes of the philosopher : it was necessary in the first place to find out what this enigma was, and to condense the problem of the world into the simplest enigmatical formula possible. The boundless am-

bition and delight of being the "unraveller of the
world" charmed the dreams of many a thinker :
nothing seemed to him worth troubling about in
this world but the means of bringing everything to
a satisfactory conclusion.   Philosophy thus became
a kind of supreme struggle for the tyrannical sway
over the intellect, and no one doubted that such a
tyrannical domination was reserved for some very
happy, subtle, ingenious, bold, and powerful person
— a single individual ! — and many (the last was
Schopenhauer) fancied themselves to be this privi-
leged person.

From this it follows that, on the whole, science
has up to the present remained in a rather back-
ward state owing to the moral narrow-mindedness
of its disciples, and that henceforth it will have to
be pursued from a higher and more generous motive.
"What do I matter ?" is written over the door of
the thinker of the future.

*　　*　　*

At the risk that moralising may also reveal itself
here as that which it has always been — namely,
resolutely *montrer ses plaies*, according to Balzac
— I would venture to protest against an improper
and injurious alteration of rank, which quite un-
noticed, and as if with the best conscience, threatens
nowadays to establish itself in the relations of science
and philosophy.   I mean to say that one must have
the right out of one's own experience — experience,
at it seems to me, always implies unfortunate experience ? — to treat of such an important question
of rank, so as not to speak of colour like the blind,
or against science like women and artists ("Ah !

this dreadful science !" sigh their instinct and their shame, "it always finds things out !") The declaration of independence of the scientific man, his emancipation from philosophy, is one of the subtler after-effects of democratic organisation and disorganisation : the self-glorification and self-conceitedness of the learned man is now everywhere in full bloom, and in its best springtime — which does not mean to imply that in this case self-praise smells sweetly. Here also the instinct of the populace cries, "Freedom from all masters !" and after science has, with the happiest results, resisted theology, whose "handmaid" it had been too long, it now proposes in its wantonness and indiscretion to lay down laws for philosophy, and in its turn to play the "master" — what am I saying ! to play the *philosopher* on its own account. My memory — the memory of a scientific man, if you please ! — teems with the naïvetés of insolence which I have heard about philosophy and philosophers from young naturalists and old physicians (not to mention the most cultured and most conceited of all learned men, the philologists and schoolmasters, who are both the one and the other by profession). On one occasion it was the specialist and the Jack Horner who instinctively stood on the defensive against all synthetic tasks and capabilities ; at another time it was the industrious worker who had got a scent of *otium* and refined luxuriousness in the internal economy of the philosopher, and felt himself aggrieved and belittled thereby. On another occasion it was the colour-blindness of the utilitarian, who sees nothing in philosophy but a series of refuted systems, and an extravagant ex-

penditure which "does nobody any good." At
another time the fear of disguised mysticism and
of the boundary-adjustment of knowledge became
conspicuous, at another time the disregard of individual philosophers, which had involuntarily ex-
tended to disregard of philosophy generally. In
fine, I found most frequently, behind the proud disdain of philosophy in young scholars, the evil after-
effect of some particular philosopher, to whom on
the whole obedience had been foresworn, without,
however, the spell of his scornful estimates of other
philosophers having been got rid of — the result being a general ill-will to all philosophy.

On the whole, speaking generally, it may just
have been the humanness, all-too-humanness of the
modern philosophers themselves, in short, their con-
temptibleness, which has injured most radically the
reverence for philosophy and opened the doors to
the instinct of the populace.   Let it but be acknowledged to what an extent our modern world diverges
from the whole style of the world of Heraclitus,
Plato, Empedocles, and whatever else all the royal
and magnificent anchorites of the spirit were called ;
and with what justice an honest man of science may
feel himself of a better family and origin, in view
of such representatives of philosophy, who, owing
to the fashion of the present day, are just as much
aloft as they are down below — in Germany, for
instance, the two lions of Berlin, the anarchist Eugen
Dühring and the amalgamist Eduard von Hartmann.
It is especially the sight of those hotch-potch philosophers, who call themselves "realists," or "positiv-
ists," which is calculated to implant a dangerous
distrust in the soul of a young and ambitious

scholar : those philosophers, at the best, are themselves but scholars and specialists, that is very evident ! All of them are persons who have been
vanquished and brought back again under the
dominion of science, who at one time or another
claimed more from themselves, without having a
right to the "more" and its responsibility — and who
now, creditably, rancorously and vindictively, represent in word and deed, *disbelief* in the master-task
and supremacy of philosophy. After all, how could
it be otherwise ? Science flourishes nowadays and
has the good conscience clearly visible on its countenance ; while that to which the entire modern
philosophy has gradually sunk, the remnant of philosophy of the present day, excites distrust and dis-
pleasure, if not scorn and pity. Philosophy reduced
to a "theory of knowledge," no more in fact than
a diffident science of epochs and doctrine of for-
bearance : a philosophy that never even gets beyond the threshold, and rigourously denies itself the
right to enter — that is philosophy in its last throes,
an end, an agony, something that awakens pity.
How could such a philosophy — rule !

I insist upon it that people finally cease confounding philosophical workers, and in general scientific
men, with philosophers — that precisely here one
should strictly give "each his own," and not give
those far too much, these far too little. It may be
necessary for the education of the real philosopher
that he himself should have once stood upon all
those steps upon which his servants, the scientific
workers of philosophy, remain standing, and must

remain standing : he himself must perhaps have been critic, and dogmatist, and historian, and besides, poet, and collector, and traveller, and riddle-reader, and moralist, and seer, and "free spirit," and almost everything, in order to traverse the whole range of human values and estimations, and that he may *be able* with a variety of eyes and consciences to look from a height to any distance, from a depth up to any height, from a nook into any expanse. But all these are only preliminary conditions for his task ; this task itself demands something else — it requires him to *create* values. The philosophical workers, after the excellent pattern of Kant and Hegel, have to fix and formalise some great existing body of valuations — that is to say, former determinations of value, creations of value, which have become prevalent, and are for a time called "truths" — whether in the domain of the *logical*, the *political* (moral), or the *artistic*. It is for these investigators to make whatever has happened and been esteemed hitherto, conspicuous, conceivable, intelligible, and manageable, to shorten everything long, even "time" itself, and to *subjugate* the entire past : an immense and wonderful task, in the carrying out of which all refined pride, all tenacious will, can surely find satisfaction. *The real philosophers, however, are commanders and law-givers ;* they say : "Thus *shall* it be !" They determine first the Whither and the Why of mankind, and thereby set aside the previous labour of all philosophical workers, and all subjugators of the past — they grasp at the future with a creative hand, and whatever is and was, becomes for them thereby a means, an instrument, and a hammer. Their "knowing" is *creating*, their creating

is a law-giving, their will to truth is — *Will to Power.*
— Are there at present such philosophers ? Have
there ever been such philosophers ? *Must* there not
be such philosophers some day ? . . .

        *   *   *

THE PROBLEM OF SOCRATES

In all ages the wisest have always agreed in their
judgment of life : it is no good. At all times and
places the same words have been on their lips, —
words full of doubt, full of melancholy, full of
weariness of life, full of hostility to life. Even
Socrates' dying words were : — "To live — means
to be ill a long while : I owe a cock to the god
Æsculapius." * Even Socrates had had enough of
it. What does that prove ? What does it point
to ? Formerly people would have said (— oh, it
has been said, and loudly enough too ; by our Pessimists loudest of all !) : "In any case there must
be some truth in this ! The *consensus sapientium*
is a proof of truth." — Shall we say the same today ?
May we do so ? "In any case there must be some
sickness here," we make reply. These great sages
of all periods should first be examined more closely !
Is it possible that they were, everyone of them, a
little shaky on their legs, effete, rocky, decadent ?
Does wisdom perhaps appear on earth after the
manner of a crow attracted by a slight smell of
carrion ?

---

* According to an ancient Greek custom, when one was cured
of an illness, he sacrificed a cock to Æsculapius in token of his
gratitude.

This irreverent belief that the great sages were decadent types, first occurred to me precisely in regard to that case concerning which both learned and vulgar prejudice was most opposed to my view. I recognised Socrates and Plato as symptoms of decline, as instruments in the disintegration of Hellas, as pseudo-Greek, as anti-Greek ("The Birth of Tragedy," 1872). That *consensus sapientium*, as I perceived ever more and more clearly, did not in the least prove that they were right in the matter on which they agreed. It proved rather that these sages themselves must have been alike in some physiological particular, in order to assume the same negative attitude towards life — in order to be bound to assume that attitude. After all, judgments and valuations of life, whether for or against, cannot be true : their only value lies in the fact that they are symptoms ; they can be considered only as symptoms, — *per se* such judgments are nonsense. You must therefore endeavour by all means to reach out and try to grasp this astonishingly subtle axiom, *that the value of life cannot be estimated.* A living man cannot do so, because he is a contending party, or rather the very object in the dispute, and not a judge ; nor can a dead man estimate it — for other reasons. For a philosopher to see a problem in the value of life, is almost an objection against him, a note of interrogation set against his wisdom — a lack of wisdom. What ? Is it possible that all these great sages were not only decadents, but that they were not even wise ? Let me however return to the problem of Socrates.

To judge from his origin, Socrates belonged to the lowest of the low : Socrates was mob. You know, and you can still see it for yourself, how ugly he was. But ugliness, which in itself is an objection, was almost a refutation among the Greeks. Was Socrates really a Greek ? Ugliness is not infrequently the expression of thwarted development, or of development arrested by crossing. In other cases it appears as a decadent development. The anthropologists among the criminal specialists declare that the typical criminal is ugly : *monstrum in fronte, monstrum in animo.* But the criminal is a decadent. Was Socrates a typical criminal ? — At all events this would not clash with that famous physiognomist's judgment which was so repugnant to Socrates' friends. While on his way through Athens a certain foreigner who was no fool at judging by looks, told Socrates to his face that he was a monster, that his body harboured all the worst vices and passions. And Socrates replied simply : "You know me, sir !" —

Not only are the acknowledged wildness and anarchy of Socrates' instincts indicative of decadence, but also that preponderance of the logical faculties and that malignity of the mis-shapen which was his special characteristic. Neither should we forget those aural delusions which were religiously interpreted as "the demon of Socrates." Everything in him is exaggerated, buffo, caricature, his nature is also full of concealment, of ulterior motives, and of underground currents. I try to understand the idiosyncrasy from which the Socratic equation : Reason = Virtue = Happiness, could have arisen : the weirdest equation ever seen, and one which was essentially opposed to all the instincts of the older Hellenes.

With Socrates Greek taste veers round in favour of dialectics : what actually occurs ? In the first place a noble taste is vanquished : with dialectics the mob comes to the top. Before Socrates' time, dialectical manners were avoided in good society : they were regarded as bad manners, they were compromising. Young men were cautioned against them. All such proffering of one's reasons was looked upon with suspicion. Honest things like honest men do not carry their reasons on their sleeve in such fashion. It is not good form to make a show of everything. That which needs to be proved cannot be worth much. Wherever authority still belongs to good usage, wherever men do not prove but command, the dialectician is regarded as a sort of clown. People laugh at him, they do not take him seriously. Socrates was a clown who succeeded in making men take him seriously : what then was the matter ?

A man resorts to dialectics only when he has no other means to hand. People know that they excite suspicion with it and that it is not very convincing. Nothing is more easily dispelled than a dialectical effect : this is proved by the experience of every gathering in which discussions are held. It can be only the last defence of those who have no other weapons. One must require to extort one's right, otherwise one makes no use of it. That is why the

Jews were dialecticians. Reynard the Fox was a
dialectician : what ? — and was Socrates one as
well ?

Is the Socratic irony an expression of revolt, of
mob resentment ?   Does Socrates, as a creature
suffering under oppression, enjoy his innate ferocity
in the knife-thrusts of the syllogism ?   Does he
wreak his revenge on the noblemen he fascinates ?
— As a dialectician a man has a merciless instrument
to wield ; he can play the tyrant with it : he compromises when he conquers with it.   The dialectician
leaves it to his opponent to prove that he is no idiot :
he infuriates, he likewise paralyses.   The dialectician cripples the intellect of his opponent.   Can it
be that dialectics was only a form of revenge in
Socrates ?

I have given you to understand in what way
Socrates was able to repel : now it is all the more
necessary to explain how he fascinated. — One reason is that he discovered a new kind of *Agon*, and
that he was the first fencing-master in the best circles
in Athens.   He fascinated by appealing to the com-
bative instinct of the Greeks, — he introduced a
variation into the contests between men and youths.
Socrates was also a great erotic.
But Socrates divined still more.   He saw right
through his noble Athenians ; he perceived that his
case, his peculiar case, was no exception even in his
time.   The same kind of degeneracy was silently
preparing itself everywhere : ancient Athens was
dying out.   And Socrates understood that the whole

world needed him, — his means, his remedy, his special artifice for self-preservation. Everywhere the instincts were in a state of anarchy ; everywhere people were within an ace of excess : the *monstrum in animo* was the general danger. "The instincts would play the tyrant ; we must discover a counter-tyrant who is stronger than they." On the occasion when that physiognomist had unmasked Socrates, and had told him what he was — a crater full of evil desires, the great Master of Irony let fall one or two words more, which provide the key to his nature. "This is true," he said, "but I overcame them all." How did Socrates succeed in mastering himself ? His case was at bottom only the extreme and most apparent example of a state of distress which was beginning to be general : that state in which no one was able to master himself and in which the instincts turned one against the other. As the extreme example of this state, he fascinated — his terrifying ugliness made him conspicuous to every eye : it is quite obvious that he fascinated still more as a reply, as a solution, as an apparent cure of this case.

When a man finds it necessary, as Socrates did, to create a tyrant out of reason, there is no small danger that something else wishes to play the tyrant. Reason was then discovered as a saviour ; neither Socrates nor his "patients" were at liberty to be rational or not, as they pleased ; at that time it was *de rigueur*, it had become a last shift. The fanaticism with which the whole of Greek thought plunges into reason, betrays a critical condition of things : men were in danger ; there were only two alternatives : either perish or else be absurdly rational. The moral bias of Greek philosophy from Plato onward, is the outcome of a pathological condition, as is also its appreciation of dialectics. Reason = Virtue = Happiness, simply means : we must imitate Socrates, and confront the dark passions permanently with the light of day — the light of reason. We must at all costs be clever, precise, clear : all yielding to the instincts, to the unconscious, leads downwards.

I have now explained how Socrates fascinated : he seemed to be a doctor, a Saviour. Is it necessary to expose the errors which lay in his faith in "reason at any price" ? — It is a piece of self-deception on the part of philosophers and moralists to suppose that they can extricate themselves from degeneration by merely waging war upon it. They cannot thus extricate themselves : that which they choose as a means, as the road to salvation, is in itself again only an expression of degeneration — they only modify its mode of manifesting itself : they do not abolish it. Socrates was a misunderstanding. *The whole of the morality of amelioration — that of Christianity as well — was a misunderstanding.* The most blinding light of day : reason at any price ; life made clear, cold, cautious, conscious, without instincts, opposed to the instincts, was in itself only a disease, another kind of disease — and by no means a return to "virtue," to "health," and to happiness. To be obliged to fight the instincts — this is the formula of degeneration : as long as life is in the ascending line, happiness is the same as instinct.

Did he understand this himself, this most intelligent of self-deceivers ? Did he confess this to himself in the end, in the wisdom of his courage before death ? Socrates wished to die. Not Athens, but his own hand gave him the draught of hemlock ; he drove Athens to the poisoned cup. "Socrates is not a doctor," he whispered to himself, "death alone can be a doctor here. . . Socrates himself has only been ill a long while."

*　*　*

I cannot here dispense with a psychology of "faith" and of the "faithful," which will naturally be to the advantage of the "faithful." If today there are still many who do not know how very *indecent* it is to be a "believer" — or to what extent such a state is the sign of decadence, and of the broken will to Life, — they will know it no later than tomorrow. My voice can make even those hear who are hard of hearing. — If perchance my ears have not deceived me, it seems that among Christians there is such a thing as a kind of criterion of truth, which is called "the proof of power." "Faith saveth ; *therefore* it is true." — It might be objected here that it is precisely salvation which is not proved but only promised : salvation is bound up with the condition "faith," — one *shall* be saved, *because* one has faith. . . . But how prove *that* that which the priest promises to the faithful really will take place, to wit : the "Beyond" which defies all demonstration ? — The assumed "proof of power" is at bottom once again only a belief in the fact that the effect which faith promises will not fail to take place. In a formula : "I believe that faith saveth ; — *consequently* it is

true." — But with this we are at the end of our
tether. This "consequently" would be the *absur-
dum* itself as a criterion of truth. — Let us be in-
dulgent enough to assume, however, that salvation
is proved by faith (— not only desired, and not
merely promised by the somewhat suspicious lips
of a priest) : could salvation — or, in technical terminology, *happiness* — ever be a proof of truth ? So
little is it so that, when pleasurable sensations make
their influence felt in replying to the question "what
is true," they furnish almost the contradiction of
truth, or at any rate they make it in the highest degree suspicious. The proof through "happiness,"
is a proof of happiness — and nothing else ; why in
the world should we take it for granted that true
judgments cause more pleasure than false ones, and
that in accordance with a pre-established harmony,
they necessarily bring pleasant feelings in their
wake ? — The experience of all strict and profound
minds teaches the reverse. Every inch of truth has
been conquered only after a struggle, almost everything to which our heart, our love and our trust in
life cleaves, has had to be sacrificed for it. Greatness of soul is necessary for this : the service of truth
is the hardest of all services. — What then is meant
by honesty in things intellectual ? It means that a
man is severe towards his own heart, that he scorns
"beautiful feelings," and that he makes a matter of
conscience out of every Yea and Nay ! — — — Faith
saveth : *consequently* it lies. . .

*   *   *

Having kept a sharp eye on philosophers, and having read between their lines long enough, I now say

to myself that the greater part of conscious thinking must be counted amongst the instinctive functions, and it is so even in the case of philosophical thinking ; one has here to learn anew, as one learned anew about heredity and "innateness." As little as the act of birth comes into consideration in the whole process and procedure of heredity, just as little is "being-conscious" opposed to the instinctive in any decisive sense ; the greater part of the conscious thinking of a philosopher is secretly influenced by his instincts, and forced into definite channels. And behind all logic and its seeming sovereignty of movement, there are valuations, or to speak more plainly, physiological demands, for the maintenance of a definite mode of life. For example, that the certain is worth more than the uncertain, that illusion is less valuable than "truth" : such valuations, in spite of their regulative importance for us, might notwithstanding be only superficial valuations, special kinds of *niaiserie*, such as may be necessary for the maintenance of beings such as ourselves. Supposing, in effect, that man is not just the "measure of things. . ."

The falseness of an opinion is not for us any objection to it : it is here, perhaps, that our new language sounds most strangely. The question is, how far an opinion is life-furthering, life-preserving, species-preserving, perhaps species-rearing ; and we are fundamentally inclined to maintain that the falsest opinions (to which the synthetic judgments *a priori* belong), are the most indispensable to us ; that without a recognition of logical fictions, without a comparison of reality with the purely imagined world of the absolute and immutable, without a con-

stant counterfeiting of the world by means of num-
bers, man could not live — that the renunciation of
false opinions would be a renunciation of life, a negation of life. *To recognise untruth as a condition of
life :* that is certainly to impugn the traditional ideas
of value in a dangerous manner, and a philosophy
which ventures to do so, has thereby alone placed
itself beyond good and evil.

It is said with good reason that convictions have
no civic rights in the domain of science : it is only
when a conviction voluntarily condescends to the
modesty of an hypothesis, a preliminary standpoint
for experiment, or a regulative fiction, that its ac-
cess to the realm of knowledge, and a certain value
therein, can be conceded, — always, however, with
the restriction that it must remain under police
supervision, under the police of our distrust. — Regarded more accurately, however, does not this imply that only when a conviction ceases to be a conviction can it obtain admission into science ? Does
not the discipline of the scientific spirit just com-
mence when one no longer harbours any conviction ? . . . It is probably so : only, it remains to be
asked whether, in order that this discipline may com-
mence, it is not necessary that there should already
be a conviction, and in fact one so imperative and
absolute, that it makes a sacrifice of all other convictions. One sees that science also rests on a belief : there is no science at all "without premises."
The question whether truth is necessary, must not
merely be affirmed beforehand, but must be affirmed
to such an extent that the principle, belief, or
conviction finds expression, that "there is nothing
more necessary than truth, and in comparison with

it everything else has only secondary value." — This
absolute will to truth : what is it ? Is it the will not
to allow ourselves to be deceived ? Is it the will
not to deceive ? For the will to truth could also be
interpreted in this fashion, provided one included
under the generalisation, "I will not deceive," the
special case, "I will not deceive myself." But why
not deceive ? Why not allow oneself to be deceived ? — Let it be noted that the reasons for the
former eventuality belong to a category quite different from those for the latter : one does not want
to be deceived oneself, under the supposition that it
is injurious, dangerous, or fatal to be deceived, —
in this sense science would be a prolonged process
of caution, foresight and utility ; against which,
however, one might reasonably make objections.
What ? is not-wishing-to-be-deceived really less injurious, less dangerous, less fatal ? What do you
know of the character of existence in all its phases
to be able to decide whether the greater advantage
is on the side of absolute distrust, or of absolute
trustfulness ? In case, however, of both being
necessary, much trusting *and* much distrusting,
whence then should science derive the absolute belief, the conviction on which it rests, that truth is
more important than anything else, even than every
other conviction ? This conviction could not have
arisen if truth and untruth had both continually
proved themselves to be useful : as is the case. Thus
— the belief in science, which now undeniably exists, cannot have had its origin in such a utilitarian
calculation, but rather *in spite of* the fact of the
inutility and dangerousness of the "Will to truth,"
of "truth at all costs," being continually demon-

strated. "At all costs" : alas, we understand that
sufficiently well, after having sacrificed and slaught-
ered one belief after another at this altar ! — Consequently, "Will to truth" does *not* imply, "I will not
allow myself to be deceived," but — there is no other
alternative — "I will not deceive, not even myself" :
and thus we have reached the realm of morality.
For, let one just ask oneself fairly : "Why wilt
thou not deceive ?" especially if it should seem —
and it does seem — as if life were laid out with a
view to appearance, I mean, with a view to error,
deceit, dissimulation, delusion, self-delusion ; and
when on the other hand it is a matter of fact that
the great type of life has always manifested itself
on the side of the most unscrupulous πολύτροποι.
Such an intention might perhaps, to express it mildly,
be a piece of Quixotism, a little enthusiastic crazi-
ness ; it might also, however, be something worse,
namely, a destructive principle, hostile to life. . .
"Will to Truth," — that might be a concealed Will
to Death. — Thus the question, Why is there science ? leads back to the moral problem : *What in
general is the purpose of morality,* if life, nature,
and history are "non-moral" ?   There is no doubt
that the conscientious man in the daring and extreme
sense in which he is presupposed by the belief in
science, affirms thereby a world other than that of
life, nature, and history ; and in so far as he affirms
this "other world," what ? must he not just thereby
— deny its counterpart, this world, our world ? . . .
But what I have in view will now be understood,
namely, that it is always a *metaphysical belief* on
which our belief in science rests, — and that even
we knowing ones of today, the godless and anti-

metaphysical, still take *our* fire from the conflagra-
tion kindled by a belief a millennium old, the Christian belief, which was also the belief of Plato, that
God is truth, that the truth is divine. . . But what
if this itself always becomes more untrustworthy,
what if nothing any longer proves itself divine, except it be error, blindness, and falsehood ; — what
if God himself turns out to be our most persistent
lie ?

* * *

I have always the same experience over again, and
always make a new effort against it ; for although it
is evident to me I do not want to believe it : *in the
greater number of men the intellectual conscience
is lacking* ; indeed, it would often seem to me that in
demanding such a thing, one is as solitary in the
largest cities as in the desert. Everyone looks at
you with strange eyes, and continues to make use of
his scales, calling this good and that bad ; and no one
blushes for shame when you remark that these
weights are not the full amount, — there is also no
indignation against you ; perhaps they laugh at your
doubt. I mean to say that *the greater number of
people* do not find it contemptible to believe this or
that, and live according to it, without having been
previously aware of the ultimate and surest reasons
for and against it, and without even giving themselves any trouble about such reasons afterwards, —
the most gifted men and the noblest women still
belong to this "greater number." But what is kind-
heartedness, refinement and genius to me, if he who
has these virtues harbours indolent sentiments in belief and judgment, if the longing for certainty does

not rule in him, as his innermost desire and profoundest need — as that which separates higher from lower men ! In certain pious people I have found a hatred of reason, and have been favourably disposed to them for it : their bad intellectual conscience at least still betrayed itself, in this manner ! But to stand in the midst of this *rerum concordia discors* and all the marvellous uncertainty and ambiguity of existence, and not to question, not to tremble with desire and delight in questioning, not even to hate the questioner — perhaps even to make merry over him to the extent of weariness — that is what I regard as contemptible, and it is this sentiment which I first of all search for in everyone : — some folly or other always persuades me anew that every man has this sentiment, as man. This is my special kind of unrighteousness.

*   *   *

Why do we fear and dread a possible return to barbarism ? Is it because it would make people less happy than they are now ? Certainly not ! the barbarians of all ages possessed more happiness than we do : let us not deceive ourselves on this point ! — but our impulse towards knowledge is too widely developed to allow us to value happiness without knowledge, or the happiness of a strong and fixed delusion : it is painful to us even to imagine such a state of things ! Our restless pursuit of discoveries and divinations has become for us as attractive and indispensable as hapless love to the lover, which on no account would he exchange for indifference, — nay, perhaps we, too, are hapless lovers ! Knowledge within us has developed into a passion, which does not shrink from any sacrifice, and at bottom fears nothing but its own extinction. We sincerely believe that all humanity, weighed down as it is by the burden of this passion, are bound to feel more exalted and comforted than formerly, when they had not yet overcome the longing for the coarser satisfaction which accompanies barbarism.

It may be that mankind may perish eventually from this passion for knowledge ! — but even that does not daunt us. Did Christianity ever shrink from a similar thought ? Are not love and death brother and sister ? Yes, we detest barbarism, — we all prefer that humanity should perish rather than that knowledge should enter into a stage of retrogression. And, finally, if mankind does not perish through some passion it will perish through some weakness : which would we prefer ? This is the main question. Do we wish its end to be in fire and light, or in the sands ?

*   *   *

Enough ! enough ! let us leave these curiosities and complexities of the modern spirit, which excite as much laughter as disgust. Our problem can certainly do without them, the problem of the meaning of the ascetic ideal — what has it got to do with yesterday or today ? those things shall be handled by me more thoroughly and severely in another connection. The only reason why I come to allude to it here is this : the ascetic ideal has at times, even in the most intellectual sphere, only one real kind of enemies and damagers : these are the comedians of this ideal — for they awake mistrust. Everywhere otherwise, where the mind is at work seriously, powerfully, and without counterfeiting, it dispenses altogether now with an ideal (the popular expression for this abstinence is "Atheism") — with the exception of the will for truth. But this will, this remnant of an ideal, is, if you will believe me, that ideal itself in its severest and cleverest formulation, esoteric through and through, stripped of all outworks, and consequently not so much its remnant as its *kernel*. Unqualified honest atheism (and its air only do we breathe, we, the most intellectual men of this age) is not opposed to that ideal, to the extent that it appears to be ; it is rather one of the final phases of its evolution, one of its syllogisms and pieces of inherent logic — it is the awe-inspiring catastrophe of a two-thousand-year training in truth, which finally forbids itself *the lie of the belief in God*. (The same course of development in India — quite independently, and consequently of some demonstrative value — the same ideal driving to the same conclusion the decisive point reached five hundred years before the European era, or more precisely at the time of Buddha — it started in the Sankhyam philosophy, and then this was popularised through Buddha, and made into a religion.)

What, I put the question with all strictness, has really triumphed over the Christian God ? The answer stands in my Joyful Wisdom, Aph. 357 : "the Christian morality itself, the idea of truth, taken as it was with increasing seriousness, the confessor-subtlety of the Christian conscience translated and sublimated into the scientific conscience into intellectual cleanness at any price. Regarding Nature as though it were a proof of the goodness and guardianship of God ; interpreting history in honour of

a divine reason, as a constant proof of a moral order
of the world and a moral teleology ; explaining our
own personal experiences, as pious men have for long
enough explained them, as though every arrangement, every nod, every single thing were invented
and sent out of love for the salvation of the soul ;
all this is now done away with, all this has the conscience against it, and is regarded by every subtler
conscience as disreputable, dishonourable, as lying,
feminism, weakness, cowardice — by means of this
severity, if by means of anything at all, are we, in
sooth, *good Europeans* and heirs of Europe's longest
and bravest self-mastery." . . . All great things go
to ruin by reason of themselves, by reason of an act
of self-dissolution : so wills the law of life, the law
of necessary "self-mastery" even in the essence of
life — ever is the law-giver finally exposed to the
cry, "*patere legem quam ipse tulisti*" ; in thus wise
did Christianity go to ruin as a dogma, through its
own morality ; in thus wise must Christianity go
again to ruin today as a morality — we are standing
on the threshold of this event. After Christian
truthfulness has drawn one conclusion after the
other, it finally draws its strongest conclusion, its
conclusion against itself ; this, however, happens,
when it puts the question, "*what is the meaning of
every will for truth ?*" And here again do I touch
on my problem, on our problem, my unknown
friends (for as yet I know of no friends) : what
sense has our whole being, if it does not mean that
in our own selves that will for truth has come to its
own consciousness *as a problem* ? — By reason of
this attainment of self-consciousness on the part of
the will for truth, morality from henceforward —

there is no doubt about it — goes to pieces : this is that great hundred-act play that *is reserved for the next two centuries of Europe, the most terrible, the most mysterious, and perhaps also the most hopeful of all plays.*

II

CRITIQUE OF CULTURE

I

THE USE AND ABUSE OF HISTORY

The unhistorical and the historical are equally necessary to the health of an individual, a community, and a system of culture.

The fact that life does need the service of history must be as clearly grasped as that an excess of history hurts it ; this will be proved later. History is necessary to the living man in three ways : in relation to his action and struggle, his conservatism and reverence, his suffering and his desire for deliverance. These three relations answer to the three kinds of history — so far as they can be distinguished — the *monumental*, the *antiquarian*, and the *critical*.

History is necessary above all to the man of action and power who fights a great fight and needs examples, teachers and comforters ; he cannot find them among his contemporaries. It was necessary in this sense to Schiller ; for our time is so evil, Goethe says, that the poet meets no nature that will profit him, among living men. To avoid being troubled by the weak and hopeless idlers, and those whose apparent activity is merely neurotic, he looks behind him and stays his course towards the goal in order to breathe. His goal is happiness, not perhaps his own, but often the nation's, or humanity's at large : he avoids quietism, and uses history as a weapon against it. For the most part he has no hope of reward except fame, which means the expectation of a niche in the temple of history, where he in his turn may be the consoler and counsellor of posterity. For his orders are that what has once been able to extend the conception "man" and give it a fairer content, must ever exist for the same office. The great moments in the individual battle form a chain, a high road for humanity through the ages, and the highest points of those vanished moments are yet great and living for men ; and this is the fundamental idea of the belief in humanity, that finds a voice in the demand for a "monumental" history.

Secondly, history is necessary to the man of conservative and reverent nature, who looks back to the origins of his existence with love and trust ; through it, he gives thanks for life. He is careful to preserve what survives from ancient days, and will reproduce the conditions of his own upbringing for those who come after him ; thus he does life a service. The possession of his ancestors' furniture changes its meaning in his soul : for his soul is rather possessed by it. All that is small and limited, mouldy and obsolete, gains a worth and inviolability of its own from the conservative and reverent soul of the antiquary migrating into it, and building a secret nest

there.   The history of his town becomes the history
of himself ; he looks on the walls, the turreted gate,
the town council, the fair, as an illustrated diary of
his youth, and sees himself in it all — his strength,
industry, desire, reason, faults and follies.   "Here
one could live," he says, "as one can live here now
— and will go on living ; for we are tough folk, and
will not be uprooted in the night."   And so, with
his "we," he surveys the marvellous individual life
of the past and identifies himself with the spirit of
the house, the family and the city.   He greets the
soul of his people from afar as his own, across the
dim and troubled centuries : his gifts and his virtues
lie in such power of feeling and divination, his scent
of a half-vanished trail, his instinctive correctness in
reading the scribbled past, and understanding at
once its palimpsests — nay, its polypsests.   Goethe
stood with such thoughts before the monument of
Erwin von Steinbach : the storm of his feeling rent
the historical cloud-veil that hung between them,
and he saw the German work for the first time
"coming from the stern, rough, German soul."   This
was the road that the Italians of the Renaissance
travelled, the spirit that reawakened the ancient
Italic genius in their poets to "a wondrous echo of
the immemorial lyre," as Jacob Burckhardt says.

There is always the danger here, that everything
ancient will be regarded as equally venerable, and
everything without this respect for antiquity, like
a new spirit, rejected as an enemy.   The Greeks
themselves admitted the archaic style of plastic art
by the side of the freer and greater style ; and later,
did not merely tolerate the pointed nose and the
cold mouth, but made them even a canon of taste.

If the judgment of a people harden in this way, and history's service to the past life be to undermine a further and higher life; if the historical sense no longer preserve life, but mummify it: then the tree dies, unnaturally, from the top downwards, and at last the roots themselves wither. Antiquarian history degenerates from the moment that it no longer gives a soul and inspiration to the fresh life of the present.

Here we see clearly how necessary a third way of looking at the past is to man, beside the other two. This is the "critical" way; which is also in the service of life. Man must have the strength to break up the past; and apply it too, in order to live. He must bring the past to the bar of judgment, interrogate it remorselessly, and finally condemn it. Every past is worth condemning: this is the rule in mortal affairs, which always contain a large measure of human power and human weakness. It is not justice that sits in judgment here; nor mercy that proclaims the verdict; but only life, the dim, driving force that insatiably desires — itself. Its sentence is always unmerciful, always unjust, as it never flows from a pure fountain of knowledge: though it would generally turn out the same, if Justice herself delivered it. "For everything that is born is worthy of being destroyed: better were it then that nothing should be born." It requires great strength to be able to live and forget how far life and injustice are one.

This is how history can serve life. Every man and nation needs a certain knowledge of the past, whether it be through monumental, antiquarian, or critical history, according to his objects, powers,

and necessities. The need is not that of the mere
thinkers who only look on at life, or the few who
desire knowledge and can only be satisfied with
knowledge ; but it has always a reference to the
end of life, and is under its absolute rule and direction. This is the natural relation of an age, a culture and a people to history ; hunger is its source,
necessity its norm, the inner plastic power assigns
its limits. The knowledge of the past is only desired for the service of the future and the present,
not to weaken the present or undermine a living
future. All this is as simple as truth itself, and quite
convincing to anyone who is not in the toils of "historical deduction."

And now to take a quick glance at our time !
We fly back in astonishment. The clearness, naturalness, and purity of the connection between life
and history has vanished ; and in what a maze of
exaggeration and contradiction do we now see the
problem ! Is the guilt ours who see it, or have life
and history really altered their conjunction and an
inauspicious star risen between them ? Others may
prove we have seen falsely ; I am merely saying
what we believe we see. There is such a star, a
bright and lordly star, and the conjunction is really
altered — by science, and the demand for history to
be a science. Life is no more dominant, and knowledge of the past no longer its thrall : boundary marks
are overthrown and everything bursts its limits.
The perspective of events is blurred, and the blur
extends through their whole immeasurable course.
No generation has seen such a panoramic comedy as
is shown by the "science of universal evolution,"

history ; that shows it with the dangerous audacity of its motto — "Fiat veritas, pereat vita."

An excess of history seems to be an enemy to the life of a time, and dangerous in five ways. Firstly, the contrast of inner and outer is emphasised and personality weakened. Secondly, the time comes to imagine that it possesses the rarest of virtues, justice, to a higher degree than any other time. Thirdly, the instincts of a nation are thwarted, the maturity of the individual arrested no less than that of the whole. Fourthly, we get the belief in the old age of mankind, the belief, at all times harmful, that we are late survivals, mere Epigoni. Lastly, an age reaches a dangerous condition of irony with regard to itself, and the still more dangerous state of cynicism, when a cunning egoistic theory of action is matured that maims and at last destroys the vital strength.

You can only explain the past by what is highest in the present. Only by straining the noblest qualities you have to their highest power will you find out what is greatest in the past, most worth knowing and preserving. Like by like ! otherwise you will draw the past to your own level. Do not believe any history that does not spring from the mind of a rare spirit. You will know the quality of the spirit, by its being forced to say something universal, or to repeat something that is known already ; the fine historian must have the power of coining the known into a thing never heard before and proclaiming the universal so simply and profoundly that the simple is lost in the profound, and the profound in the simple.

The unrestrained historical sense, pushed to its logical extreme, uproots the future, because it destroys illusions and robs existing things of the only atmosphere in which they can live. Historical justice, even if practised conscientiously, with a pure heart, is therefore a dreadful virtue, because it always undermines and ruins the living thing : its judgment always means annihilation. If there be no constructive impulse behind the historical one, if the clearance of rubbish be not merely to leave the ground free for the hopeful living future to build its house, if justice alone be supreme, the creative instinct is sapped and discouraged. A religion, for example, that has to be turned into a matter of historical knowledge by the power of pure justice, and to be scientifically studied throughout, is destroyed at the end of it all. For the historical audit brings so much to light which is false and absurd, violent and inhuman, that the condition of pious illusion falls to pieces. And a thing can only live through a pious illusion. For man is creative only through love and in the shadow of love's illusions, only through the unconditional belief in perfection and righteousness. Everything that forces a man to be no longer unconditioned in his love, cuts at the root of his strength : he must wither, and be dishonoured. Art has the opposite effect to history : and only perhaps if history suffer transformation into a pure work of art, can it preserve instincts or arouse them. Such history would be quite against the analytical and inartistic tendencies of our time, and even be considered false. But the history that merely destroys without any impulse to construct, will in the long run make its instruments tired of life ; for such men destroy illusions, and "he who destroys illusions in himself and others is punished by the ultimate tyrant, Nature."

The belief that one is a late-comer in the world is, anyhow, harmful and degrading : but it must appear frightful and devastating when it raises our late-comer to godhead, by a neat turn of the wheel, as the true meaning and object of all past creation, and his conscious misery is set up as the perfection of the world's history. Such a point of view has accustomed the Germans to talk of a "world-process," and justify their own time as its necessary result. And it has put history in the place of the other spiritual powers, art and religion, as the one sovereign ; inasmuch as it is the "Idea realising itself," the "Dialectic of the spirit of the nations," and the "tribunal of the world."

History understood in this Hegelian way has been contemptuously called God's sojourn upon earth, — though the God was first created by the history. He, at any rate, became transparent and intelligible inside Hegelian skulls, and has risen through all the dialectically possible steps in his being up to the manifestation of the Self : so that for Hegel the highest and final stage of the world-process came together in his own Berlin existence. He ought to have said that everything after him was merely to be regarded as the musical coda of the great historical rondo, — or rather, as simply superfluous. He has not said it ; and thus he has implanted in a generation leavened throughout by him the worship of the "power of history," that practically turns every moment into a sheer gaping at success, into an idolatry of the actual : for which we have now discovered the characteristic phrase "to adapt ourselves to circumstances." But the man who has once learnt to crook the knee and bow the head before the power of history, nods "yes" at last, like a Chinese doll, to every power, whether it be a government or a public opinion or a numerical majority ; and his limbs move correctly as the power pulls the string. If each success have come by a "rational necessity," and every event show the victory of logic or the "Idea," then — down on your knees quickly, and let every step in the ladder of success have its reverence ! There are no more living mythologies, you say ? Religions are at their last gasp ? Look at the religion of the power of history, and the priests of the mythology of Ideas, with their scarred knees ! Do not all the virtues follow in the train of the new faith ? And shall we not call it unselfishness, when the historical man lets himself be turned into an "objective" mirror of all that is ? Is it not magnanimity to renounce all power in heaven and earth in order to adore the mere fact of power ? Is it not justice, always to hold the balance of forces in your hands and observe which is the stronger and heavier ? And what a school of politeness is such a contemplation of the past ! To take everything objectively, to be angry at nothing, to love nothing, to understand everything — makes one gentle and pliable. Even if a man brought up in this school will show himself openly offended, one is just as pleased, knowing it is only meant in the artistic sense of *ira et studium*, though it is really *sine ira et studio*.

What old-fashioned thoughts I have on such a combination of virtue and mythology ! But they must out, however one may laugh at them. I would even say that history always teaches — "it was once," and morality — "it ought not to be, or have been." So history becomes a compendium of actual immorality. But how wrong would one be to regard history as the judge of this actual immorality! Morality is offended by the fact that a Raphael had to die at thirty-six ; such a being ought not to die. If you came to the help of history, as the apologists of the actual, you would say : "he had spoken everything that was in him to speak, a longer life would only have enabled him to create a similar beauty, and not a new beauty," and so on. Thus you become an *advocatus diaboli* by setting up the success, the fact, as your idol : whereas the fact is always dull, at all times more like a calf than a god.

Excess of history has attacked the plastic power of life, that no more understands how to use the past as a means of strength and nourishment. It is a fearful disease, and yet, if youth had not a natural gift for clear vision, no one would see that it is a disease, and that a paradise of health has been lost. But the same youth, with that same natural instinct of health, has guessed how the paradise can be regained. It knows the magic herbs and simples for the malady of history, and the excess of it. And what are they called ?

It is no marvel that they bear the names of poisons : — the antidotes to history are the "unhistorical" and the "super-historical." With these names we return to the beginning of our inquiry and draw near to its final close.

By the word "unhistorical" I mean the power, the art of forgetting, and of drawing a limited horizon round one's self. I call the power "super-historical" which turns the eyes from the process of becoming to that which gives existence an eternal and stable character, to art and religion. Science — for it is science that makes us speak of "poisons" — sees in these powers contrary powers : for it considers only that view of things to be true and right, and therefore scientific, which regards something as finished and historical, not as continuing and eternal. Thus it lives in a deep antagonism towards the powers that make for eternity — art and religion, — for it hates the forgetfulness that is the death of knowledge, and tries to remove all limitation of horizon and cast men into an infinite boundless sea, whose waves are bright with the clear knowledge — of becoming !

If they could only live therein ! Just as towns are shaken by an avalanche and become desolate, and man builds his house there in fear and for a season only ; so life is broken in sunder and becomes weak and spiritless, if the avalanche of ideas started by science take from man the foundation of his rest and security, the belief in what is stable and eternal. Must life dominate knowledge, or knowledge life ? Which of the two is the higher, and decisive power ? There is no room for doubt : life is the higher, and the dominating power, for the knowledge that annihilated life would be itself annihilated too. Knowledge presupposes life, and has the same interest in maintaining it that every creature has in its own preservation. Science needs very careful watching : there is a hygiene of life near the volumes of science, and one of its sentences runs thus : — The unhistorical and the super-historical are the natural antidotes against the overpowering of life by history; they are the cures for the historical disease. We who are sick of the disease may suffer a little from the antidote. But this is no proof that the treatment we have chosen is wrong.

And here I see the mission of the youth that forms the first generation of fighters and dragon-slayers : it will bring a more beautiful and blessed humanity and culture, but will have itself no more than a glimpse of the promised land of happiness and wondrous beauty. This youth will suffer both from the malady and its antidotes : and yet it believes in strength and health and boasts a nature closer to the great Nature than its forebears, the cultured men and graybeards of the present. But its mission is to shake to their foundations the present conceptions of "health" and "culture," and erect hatred and scorn in the place of this rococo mass of ideas. And the clearest sign of its own strength and health is just the fact that it can use no idea, no party-cry from the present-day mint of words and ideas to symbolise its own existence : but only claims conviction from the power in it that acts and fights, breaks up and destroys ; and from an ever heightened feeling of life when the hour strikes. You may deny this youth any culture — but how would youth count that a reproach ? You may speak of its rawness and intemperateness — but it is not yet old and wise enough to be acquiescent. It need not pretend to a ready-made culture at all ; but enjoys all the rights — and the consolations — of youth, especially the right of brave unthinking honesty and the consolation of an inspiring hope.

How can we reach that end ? you will ask. The

Delphian god cries his oracle to you at the beginning of your wanderings, "Know thyself." It is a
hard saying : for that god "tells nothing and conceals nothing but merely points the way," as Heraclitus said. But whither does he point?

In certain epochs the Greeks were in a similar
danger of being overwhelmed by what was past
and foreign, and perishing on the rock of "history."
They never lived proud and untouched. Their
"culture" was for a long time a chaos of foreign
forms and ideas, — Semitic, Babylonian, Lydian and
Egyptian, — and their religion a battle of all the
gods of the East ; just as German culture and religion is at present a death-struggle of all foreign nations and bygone times. And yet, Hellenic culture
was no mere mechanical unity, thanks to that
Delphic oracle. The Greeks gradually learned to
organise the chaos, by taking Apollo's advice and
thinking back to themselves, to their own true necessities, and letting all the sham necessities go. Thus
they again came into possession of themselves, and
did not remain long the Epigoni of the whole East,
burdened with their inheritance. After that hard
fight, they increased and enriched the treasure they
had inherited by their obedience to the oracle, and
they became the ancestors and models for all the cultured nations of the future.

This is a parable for each one of us : he must
organise the chaos in himself by "thinking himself
back" to his true needs. He will want all his honesty, all the sturdiness and sincerity in his character
to help him to revolt against second-hand thought,
second-hand learning, second-hand action. And he
will begin then to understand that culture can be

something more than a "decoration of life" — a concealment and disfiguring of it, in other words ; for
all adornment hides what is adorned.   And thus the
Greek idea, as against the Roman, will be discovered
to him, the idea of culture as a new and finer nature,
without distinction of inner and outer, without convention or disguise, as a unity of thought and will,
life and appearance.   He will learn too, from his
own experience, that it was by a greater force of
moral character that the Greeks were victorious,
and that everything which makes for sincerity is a
further step towards true culture, however this sincerity may harm the ideals of education that are
reverenced at the time, or even have power to shat-
ter a whole system of merely decorative culture.

                    *   *   *

                         2

            EUROPE, THE GERMANS, WAGNER

   Let us examine another aspect of the question :
it is not only obvious that German culture is declining, but adequate reasons for this decline are not
lacking.   After all, nobody can spend more than he
has : — this is true of individuals, it is also true of
nations.   If you spend your strength in acquiring
power, or in politics on a large scale, or in economy,
or in universal commerce, or in parliamentarism, or
in military interests — if you dissipate the modicum
of reason, of earnestness, of will, and of self-control
that constitutes your nature in one particular fashion, you cannot dissipate it in another.   Culture and
the state — let no one be deceived on this point —
are antagonists : A "culture-state" is merely a mod-

ern idea. The one lives upon the other, the one flourishes at the expense of the other. All great periods of culture have been periods of political decline ; that which is great from the standpoint of culture, was always unpolitical — even anti-political. Goethe's heart opened at the coming of Napoleon — it closed at the thought of the "Wars of Liberation." At the very moment when Germany arose as a great power in the world of politics, France won new importance as a force in the world of culture. Even at this moment a large amount of fresh intellectual earnestness and passion has emigrated to Paris ; the question of pessimism, for instance, and the question of Wagner ; in France almost all psychological and artistic questions are considered with incomparably more subtlety and thoroughness than they are in Germany, — the Germans are even incapable of this kind of earnestness. In the history of European culture the rise of the Empire signifies, above all, a displacement of the centre of gravity. Everywhere people are already aware of this : in things that really matter — and these after all constitute culture, — the Germans are no longer worth considering. I ask you, can you show me one single man of brains who could be mentioned in the same breath with other European thinkers, like your Goethe, your Hegel, your Heinrich Heine, and your Schopenhauer ? — The fact that there is no longer a single German philosopher worth mentioning is an increasing wonder.

I have spoken of German intellect. I have said that it is becoming coarser and shallower. Is that enough ? — In reality something very different frightens me, and that is the ever steady decline of German earnestness, German profundity, and German passion in things intellectual. Not only intellectuality, but also pathos has altered. From time to time I come in touch with German universities ; what an extraordinary atmosphere prevails among their scholars ! what barrenness'! and what self-satisfied and lukewarm intellectuality ! For any one to point to German science as an argument against me would show that he grossly misunderstood my meaning, while it would also prove that he had not read a word of my writings. For seventeen years I have done little else than expose the de-intellectualising influence of our modern scientific studies. The severe slavery to which every individual nowadays is condemned by the enormous range covered by the sciences, is the chief reason why fuller, richer and profounder natures can find no education or educators that are fit for them. Nothing is more deleterious to this age than the superfluity of pretentious loafers and fragmentary human beings ; our universities are really the involuntary forcing houses for this kind of withering-up of the instincts of intellectuality. And the whole of Europe is beginning to know this — politics on a large scale deceive no one. Germany is becoming ever more and more the Flat-land of Europe. I am still in search of a German with whom I could be serious after my own fashion. And how much more am I in search of one with whom I could be cheerful. — The Twilight of the Idols : ah! what man today would be capable of understanding the kind of seriousness from which a philosopher is recovering in this work ! It is our cheerfulness that people understand least.

Goethe. — No mere German, but a European
event : a magnificent attempt to overcome the eighteenth century by means of a return to nature, by
means of an ascent to the naturalness of the Renaissance, a kind of self-overcoming on the part of the
century in question. — He bore the strongest instincts of this century in his breast : its sentimental-
ity, and idolatry of nature, its anti-historic, idealistic,
unreal, and revolutionary spirit (— the latter is only
a form of the unreal). He enlisted history, natural
science, antiquity, as well as Spinoza, and above all
practical activity, in his service. He drew a host
of very definite horizons around him ; far from
liberating himself from life, he plunged right into
it ; he did not give in ; he took as much as he could
on his own shoulders, and into his heart. That to
which he aspired was totality ; he was opposed to
the sundering of reason, sensuality, feeling and will
(as preached with most repulsive scholasticism by
Kant, the antipodes of Goethe) ; he disciplined himself into a harmonious whole, he *created* himself.
Goethe in the midst of an age of unreal sentiment,
was a convinced realist : he said yea to everything
that was like him in this regard, — there was no
greater event in his life than that *ens realissimum*,
surnamed Napoleon. Goethe conceived a strong,
highly-cultured man, skilful in all bodily accomplishments, able to keep himself in check, having a
feeling of reverence for himself, and so constituted
as to be able to risk the full enjoyment of naturalness in all its rich profusion and be strong enough
for this freedom ; a man of tolerance, not out of
weakness but out of strength, because he knows
how to turn to his own profit that which would

ruin the mediocre nature ; a man unto whom nothing is any longer forbidden, unless it be weakness
either as a vice or as a virtue.   Such a spirit, *become
free*, appears in the middle of the universe with a
feeling of cheerful and confident fatalism ; he believes that only individual things are bad, and that
as a whole the universe justifies and affirms itself —
He no longer denies. . . But such a faith is the highest of all faiths : I christened it with the name of
Dionysus.

We "good Europeans," we also have hours when
we allow ourselves a warm-hearted patriotism, a
plunge and relapse into old loves and narrow views
— I have just given an example of it — hours of national excitement, of patriotic anguish, and all other
sorts of old-fashioned floods of sentiment.   Duller
spirits may perhaps only get done with what con-
fines its operations in us to hours and plays itself out
in hours — in a considerable time : some in half a
year, others in half a lifetime, according to the speed
and strength with which they digest and "change
their material."   Indeed, I could think of sluggish,
hesitating races, which even in our rapidly moving
Europe, would require half a century ere they could
surmount such atavistic attacks of patriotism and
soil-attachment, and return once more to reason,
that is to say, to "good Europeanism."   And while
digressing on this possibility, I happened to become
an ear-witness of a conversation between two old
patriots — they were evidently both hard of hearing and consequently spoke all the louder.   "He
has as much, and knows as much, philosophy as a

peasant or a corps-student," said the one — "he is still innocent. But what does that matter nowadays ! It is the age of the masses : they lie on their belly before everything that is massive. And so also *in politicis.* A statesman who rears up for them a new Tower of Babel, some monstrosity of empire and power, they call 'great' — what does it matter that we more prudent and conservative ones do not meanwhile give up the old belief that it is only the great thought that gives greatness to an action or affair. Supposing a statesman were to bring his people into the position of being obliged henceforth to practise 'high politics,' for which they were by nature badly endowed and prepared, so that they would have to sacrifice their old and reliable virtues, out of love to a new and doubtful mediocrity ; — supposing a statesman were to condemn his people generally to 'practise politics,' when they have hitherto had something better to do and think about, and when in the depths of their souls they have been unable to free themselves from a prudent loathing of the restlessness, emptiness, and noisy wranglings of the essentially politics-practising nations ; — supposing such a statesman were to stimulate the slumbering passions and avidities of his people, were to make a stigma out of their former diffidence and delight in aloofness, an offence out of their exoticism and hidden permanency, were to depreciate their most radical proclivities, subvert their consciences, make their minds narrow, and their tastes 'national' — what ! a statesman who should do all this, which his people would have to do penance for throughout their whole future, if they had a future, such a statesman would be great, would he ?" — "Undoubt-

edly !" replied the other old patriot vehemently ;
"otherwise he *could not* have done it ! It was mad
perhaps to wish such a thing ! But perhaps everything great has been just as mad at its commence-
ment !" — "Misuse of words !" cried his interlocutor,
contradictorily — "strong ! strong ! Strong and
mad ! *Not* great !" — The old men had obviously
become heated as they thus shouted their "truths" in
each other's faces ; but I, in my happiness and apart-
ness, considered how soon a stronger one may become master of the strong ; and also that there is a
compensation for the intellectual superficialising of a
nation — namely, in the deepening of another.

Whether we call it "civilisation," or "humanis-
ing," or "progress," which now distinguishes the
European ; whether we call it simply, without praise
or blame, by the political formula : the *democratic*
movement in Europe — behind all the moral and
political foregrounds pointed to by such formulas,
an immense physiological process goes on, which is
ever extending : the process of the assimilation of
Europeans ; their increasing detachment from the
conditions under which, climatically and hereditar-
ily, united races originate ; their increasing independence of every definite *milieu*, that for centuries
would fain inscribe itself with equal demands on
soul and body ; — that is to say, the slow emergence
of an essentially *super-national* and nomadic species
of man, who possesses, physiologically speaking, a
maximum of the art and power of adaptation as his
typical distinction. This process of the *evolving
European*, which can be retarded in its tempo by

great relapses, but will perhaps just gain and grow thereby in vehemence and depth — the still raging storm and stress of "national sentiment" pertains to it, and also the anarchism which is appearing at present — this process will probably arrive at results on which its naïve propagators and panegyrists, the apostles of "modern ideas," would least care to reckon. The same new conditions under which on an average a levelling and mediocrising of man will take place — a useful, industrious, variously serviceable and clever gregarious man — are in the highest degree suitable to give rise to exceptional men of the most dangerous and attractive qualities. For, while the capacity for adaptation, which is every day trying changing conditions, and begins a new work with every generation, almost with every decade, makes the *powerfulness* of the type impossible ; while the collective impression of such future Europeans will probably be that of numerous, talkative, weak-willed, and very handy workmen who *require* a master, a commander, as they require their daily bread ; while, therefore, the democratising of Europe will tend to the production of a type prepared for *slavery* in the most subtle sense of the term : the strong man will necessarily in individual and exceptional cases, become stronger and richer than he has perhaps ever been before — owing to the unprejudicedness of his schooling, owing to the immense variety of practice, art, and disguise. I meant to say that the democratising of Europe is at the same time an involuntary arrangement for the rearing of tyrants — taking the word in all its meanings, even in its most spiritual sense.

The German soul is above all manifold, varied in its source, aggregated and superimposed, rather than actually built : this is owing to its origin. A German who would embolden himself to assert : "Two souls, alas, dwell in my breast," would make a bad guess at the truth, or, more correctly, he would come far short of the truth about the number of souls. As a people made up of the most extraordinary mixing and mingling of races, perhaps even with a preponderance of the pre-Aryan element, as the "people of the centre" in every sense of the term, the Germans are more intangible, more ample, more contradictory, more unknown, more incalculable, more surprising, and even more terrifying than other peoples are to themselves : — they escape definition, and are thereby alone the despair of the French. It is characteristic of the Germans that the question : "What is German ?" never dies out among them.

* * *

What Europe owes to the Jews ? — Many things, good and bad, and above all one thing of the nature both of the best and the worst : the grand style in morality, the fearfulness and majesty of infinite demands, of infinite significations, the whole Romanticism and sublimity of moral questionableness — and consequently just the most attractive, ensnaring, and exquisite element in those iridescences and allurements to life, in the aftersheen of which the sky of our European culture, its evening sky, now glows — perhaps glows out. For this, we artists among the spectators and philosophers, are — grateful to the Jews.

* * *

Finally, let it not be forgotten that the English
with their profound mediocrity, brought about once
before a general depression of European intelligence.
What is called "modern ideas," or "the ideas of the
eighteenth century," or "French ideas" — that, consequently, against which the German mind rose up
with profound disgust — is of English origin, there
is no doubt about it. The French were only the
apes and actors of these ideas, their best soldiers, and
likewise, alas ! their first and profoundest victims ;
for owing to the diabolical Anglomania of "modern
ideas," the *âme français* has in the end become so
thin and emaciated, that at present one recalls its
sixteenth and seventeenth centuries, its profound,
passionate strength, its inventive excellency, almost
with disbelief. One must, however, maintain this
verdict of historical justice in a determined manner, and defend it against present prejudices and appearances : the European *noblesse* — of sentiment,
taste, and manners, taking the word in every high
sense — is the work and invention of France ; the
European ignobleness, the plebeianism of modern
ideas — is England's work and invention.

Even at present France is still the seat of the most
intellectual and refined culture of Europe, it is still
the high school of taste ; but one must know how
to find this "France of taste." He who belongs to
it keeps himself well concealed : — they may be a
small number in whom it lives and is embodied, besides perhaps being men who do not stand upon the
strongest legs, in part fatalists, hypochondriacs, in-
valids, in part persons over-indulged, over-refined,
such as have the ambition to conceal themselves.
They have all something in common : they keep

their ears closed in presence of the delirious folly and noisy spouting of the democratic *bourgeois*. In fact, a besotted and brutalised France at present sprawls in the foreground — it recently celebrated a veritable orgy of bad taste, and at the same time of self-admiration, at the funeral of Victor Hugo. There is also something else common to them : a predilection to resist intellectual Germanising — and a still greater inability to do so ! In this France of intellect, which is also a France of pessimism, Schopenhauer has perhaps become more at home, and more indigenous than he has ever been in Germany ; not to speak of Heinrich Heine, who has long ago been re-incarnated in the more refined and fastidious lyrists of Paris ; or of Hegel, who at present, in the form of Taine — the first of living historians — exercises an almost tyrannical influence. As regards Richard Wagner, however, the more French music learns to adapt itself to the actual needs of the *âme moderne*, the more will it "Wagnerise" ; one can safely predict that beforehand, — it is already taking place sufficiently ! There are, however, three things which the French can still boast of with pride as their heritage and possession, and as indelible tokens of their ancient intellectual superiority in Europe, in spite of all voluntary or involuntary Germanising and vulgarising of taste. Firstly, the capacity for artistic emotion, for devotion to "form," for which the expression, *l'art pour l'art*, along with numerous others, has been invented : — such capacity has not been lacking in France for three centuries ; and owing to its reverence for the "small number," it has again and again made a sort of chamber music of literature possible, which is sought for in vain elsewhere in Europe. — The second thing whereby the French can lay claim to a superiority over Europe is their ancient, many-sided, *moralistic* culture, owing to which one finds on an average, even in the petty *romanciers* of the newspapers and chance *boule-vardiers de Paris*, a psychological sensitiveness and curiosity, of which, for example, one has no concep-tion (to say nothing of the thing itself !) in Ger-many. The Germans lack a couple of centuries of the moralistic work requisite thereto, which, as we have said, France has not grudged : those who call the Germans "naïve" on that account give them commendation for a defect. (As the opposite of the German inexperience and innocence *in volup-tate psychologica*, which is not too remotely asso-ciated with the tediousness of German intercourse, — and as the most successful expression of genuine French curiosity and inventive talent in this domain of delicate thrills, Henri Beyle [Stendhal] may be noted ; that remarkable anticipatory and forerun-ning man, who, with a Napoleonic *tempo*, traversed his Europe, in fact, several centuries of the European soul, as a surveyor and discoverer thereof : — it has required two generations to overtake him one way or other, to divine long afterwards some of the rid-dles that perplexed and enraptured him — this strange Epicurean and man of interrogation, the last great psychologist of France.) — There is yet a third claim to superiority : in the French character there is a successful half-way synthesis of the North and South, which makes them comprehend many things, and enjoins upon them other things, which an Eng-lishman can never comprehend. Their tempera-ment, turned alternately to and from the South, in which from time to time the Provençal and Ligurian blood froths over, preserves them from the dreadful, northern grey-in-grey, from sunless conceptual-spectrism and from poverty of blood — our German infirmity of taste, for the excessive prevalence of which at the present moment, blood and iron, that is to say "high politics," has with great resolution been prescribed (according to a dangerous healing art, which bids me wait and wait, but not yet hope). — There is also still in France a pre-understanding and ready welcome for those rarer and rarely gratified men, who are too comprehensive to find satisfaction in any kind of fatherlandism, and know how to love the South when in the North and the North when in the South — the born Midlanders, the "good Europeans." For them Bizet has made music, this latest genius, who has seen a new beauty and seduction, — who has discovered a piece of the *South in music*.

Owing to the morbid estrangement which the nationality-craze has induced and still induces among the nations of Europe, owing also to the short-sighted and hasty-handed politicians, who with the help of this craze, are at present in power, and do not suspect to what extent the disintegrating policy they pursue must necessarily be only an interlude policy — owing to all this, and much else that is altogether unmentionable at present, the most unmistakable signs that Europe wishes to be one, are now overlooked, or arbitrarily and falsely misinterpreted. With all the more profound and large-minded men of this century, the real general tendency of the mysterious labour of their souls was to prepare the way for that new synthesis, and tentatively to antici-

pate the European of the future ; only in their simu-
lations, or in their weaker moments, in old age perhaps, did they belong to the "fatherlands" — they
only rested from themselves when they became
"patriots." I think of such men as Napoleon,
Goethe, Beethoven, Stendhal, Heinrich Heine,
Schopenhauer : it must not be taken amiss if I also
count Richard Wagner among them, about whom
one must not let oneself be deceived by his own misunderstandings (geniuses like him have seldom the
right to understand themselves), still less, of course,
by the unseemly noise with which he is now resisted
and opposed in France : the fact remains, nevertheless, that Richard Wagner and the later French Romanticism of the forties, are most closely and in-
timately related to one another. They are akin,
fundamentally akin, in all the heights and depths of
their requirements ; it is Europe, the one Europe,
whose soul presses urgently and longingly, outwards
and upwards, in their multifarious and boisterous
art — whither ? into a new light ? towards a new
sun ?   But who would attempt to express accurately
what all these masters of new modes of speech could
not express distinctly ?   It is certain that the same
storm and stress tormented them, that they sought
in the same manner, these last great seekers !   All
of them steeped in literature to their eyes and ears —
the first artists of universal literary culture — for the
most part even themselves writers, poets, interme-
diaries and blenders of the arts and the senses (Wagner, as musician is reckoned among painters, as poet
among musicians, as artist generally among actors);
all of them fanatics for expression "at any cost" —
I specially mention Delacroix, the nearest related to

Wagner ; all of them great discoverers in the realm
of the sublime, also of the loathsome and dreadful,
still greater discoverers in effect, in display, in the art
of the show-shop ; all of them talented far beyond
their genius, out and out *virtuosi*, with mysterious
accesses to all that seduces, allures, constrains, and
upsets ; born enemies of logic and of the straight line,
hankering after the strange, the exotic, the mon-
strous, the crooked, and the self-contradictory ; as
men, Tantaluses of the will, plebeian parvenus, who
knew themselves to be incapable of a noble *tempo*
or of a *lento* in life and action — think of Balzac,
for instance, — unrestrained workers, almost de-
stroying themselves by work ; antinomians and reb-
els in manners, ambitious and insatiable, without
equilibrium and enjoyment ; all of them finally shat-
tering and sinking down at the Christian cross (and
with right and reason, for who of them would have
been sufficiently profound and sufficiently original
for an *Antichristian* philosophy ?) ; — on the whole,
a boldly daring, splendidly overbearing, high-flying,
and aloft-up-dragging class of higher men, who had
first to teach their century — and it is the century of
the *masses* — the conception "higher man." . . . Let
the German friends of Richard Wagner advise together as to whether there is anything purely German in the Wagnerian art, or whether its distinction
does not consist precisely in coming from *super-*
German sources and impulses : in which connection
it may not be underrated how indispensable Paris
was to the development of his type, which the
strength of his instincts made him long to visit at
the most decisive time — and how the whole style of
his proceedings, of his self-apostolate, could only

perfect itself in sight of the French socialistic original. On a more subtle comparison it will perhaps
be found, to the honour of Richard Wagner's German nature, that he has acted in everything with
more strength, daring, severity, and elevation than
a nineteenth-century Frenchman could have done —
owing to the circumstance that we Germans are as
yet nearer to barbarism than the French ; — perhaps
even the most remarkable creation of Richard Wagner is not only at present, but for ever inaccessible,
incomprehensible, and inimitable to the whole latter-
day Latin race : the figure of Siegfried, that *very
free* man, who is probably far too free, too hard,
too cheerful, too healthy, too anti-Catholic for the
taste of old and mellow civilised nations. He may
even have been a sin against Romanticism, this anti-
Latin Siegfried : well, Wagner atoned amply for
this sin in his old sad days, when — anticipating a
taste which has meanwhile passed into politics — he
began, with the religious vehemence peculiar to him,
to preach, at least, *the way to Rome*, if not to walk
therein.

*   *   *

I believe that artists very often do not know what
they are best able to do.   They are much too vain.
Their minds are directed to something prouder than
merely to appear like little plants, which, with freshness, rareness, and beauty, know how to sprout from
their soil with real perfection. The ultimate goodness of their own garden and vineyard is super-
ciliously under-estimated by them, and their love
and their insight are not of the same quality. Here
is a musician who is a greater master than anyone

else in the discovering of tones, peculiar to suffering, oppressed, and tormented souls, who can endow even dumb misery with speech. Nobody can approach him in the colours of late autumn, in the indescribably touching joy of a last, a very last, and all too short gladness ; he knows of a chord which expresses those secret and weird midnight hours of the soul, when cause and effect seem to have fallen asunder, and at every moment something may spring out of nonentity. He is happiest of all when creating from out the nethermost depths of human happiness, and, so to speak, from out man's empty bumper, in which the bitterest and most repulsive drops have mingled with the sweetest for good or evil at last. He knows that weary shuffling along of the soul which is no longer able either to spring or to fly, nay, which is no longer able to walk ; he has the modest glance of concealed suffering, of understanding without comfort, of leave-taking without word or sign ; verily as the Orpheus of all secret misery he is greater than anyone, and many a thing was introduced into art for the first time by him, which hitherto had not been given expression, had not even been thought worthy of art — the cynical revolts, for instance, of which only the greatest sufferer is capable, also many a small and quite microscopical feature of the soul, as it were the scales of its amphibious nature — yes indeed, he is the master of everything very small. But this he refuses to be ! His tastes are much more in love with vast walls and with daring frescoes ! . . . He does not see that his spirit has another desire and bent — a totally different outlook — that it prefers to squat peacefully in the corners of broken-down houses: concealed in this way, and hidden even from himself, he paints his really great masterpieces, all of which are very short, often only one bar in length — there, only, does he become quite good, great and perfect, perhaps there alone. — Wagner is one who has suffered much — and this elevates him above other musicians. — I admire Wagner wherever he sets himself to music.

The artist of decadence. That is the word. And here I begin to be serious. I could not think of looking on approvingly while this *décadent* spoils our health — and music into the bargain. Is Wagner a man at all? Is he not rather a disease? Everything he touches he contaminates. He has made music sick.

Wagner is a great corrupter of music. With it, he found the means of stimulating tired nerves, — and in this way he made music ill. In the art of spurring exhausted creatures back into activity, and of recalling half-corpses to life, the inventiveness he shows is of no mean order. He is the master of hypnotic trickery, and he fells the strongest like bullocks. Wagner's success — his success with nerves, and therefore with women — converted the whole world of ambitious musicians into disciples of his secret art. And not only the ambitious, but also the *shrewd*. . . Only with morbid music can money be made today; our big theatres live on Wagner.

Taking everything into consideration, I could never have survived my youth without Wagnerian music. For I was condemned to the society of

Germans. If a man wish to get rid of a feeling of insufferable oppression, he has to take to hashish. Well, I had to take to Wagner. Wagner is the counter-poison to everything essentially German — the fact that he is a poison too, I do not deny.

The curiosity of the psychologist is so great in me, that I regard it as quite a special privilege to have lived at the right time, and to have lived precisely among Germans, in order to be ripe for this work. The world must indeed be empty for him who has never been unhealthy enough for this "infernal voluptuousness" : it is allowable, it is even imperative, to employ a mystic formula for this purpose. I suppose I know better than any one the prodigious feats of which Wagner was capable, the fifty worlds of strange ecstasies to which no one else had wings to soar ; and as I am alive today and strong enough to turn even the most suspicious and most dangerous things to my own advantage, and thus to grow stronger, I declare Wagner to have been the greatest benefactor of my life. The bond which unites us is the fact that we have suffered greater agony, even at each other's hands, than most men are able to bear nowadays, and this will always keep our names associated in the minds of men. For, just as Wagner is merely a misunderstanding among Germans, so, in truth, am I, and ever will be. Ye lack two centuries of psychological and artistic discipline, my dear countrymen ! . . . But ye can never recover the time lost.

* * *

But here nothing shall stop me from being rude, and from telling the Germans one or two unpleasant home truths : who else would do it if I did not ? I refer to their laxity in matters historical. Not only have the Germans entirely lost the *breadth of vision* which enables one to grasp the course of culture and the values of culture ; not only are they one and all political (or Church) puppets ; but they have also actually put a ban upon this very breadth of vision. A man must first and foremost be "German," he must belong to "*the* race" ; then only can he pass judgment upon all values and lack of values in history — then only can he establish them. . . To be German is in itself an argument, "Germany, Germany above all," is a principle ; the Germans stand for the "moral order of the universe" in history ; compared with the Roman Empire, they are the upholders of freedom ; compared with the eighteenth century, they are the restorers of morality, of the "Categorical Imperative." There is such a thing as the writing of history according to the lights of Imperial Germany ; there is, I fear, anti-Semitic history — there is also history written with an eye to the Court, and Herr von Treitschke is not ashamed of himself. Quite recently an idiotic opinion *in historicis*, an observation of Vischer the Swabian æsthete, since happily deceased, made the round of the German newspapers as a "truth" to which every German must assent. The observation was this : "The Renaissance and the Reformation only together constitute a whole — the æsthetic rebirth, and the moral rebirth." When I listen to such things, I lose all patience, and I feel inclined, I even feel it my duty, to tell the Germans, for once in a way, all that they have on their conscience. *Every great crime against culture for the last four centuries lies on their conscience.* . . And always for the same reason, always owing to their bottomless cowardice in the face of reality, which is also cowardice in the face of truth ; always owing to the love of falsehood which has become almost instinctive in them — in short, "idealism." It was the Germans who caused Europe to lose the fruits, the whole meaning of her last period of greatness — the period of the Renaissance. At a moment when a higher order of values, values that were noble, that said yea to life, and that guaranteed a future, had succeeded in triumphing over the opposite values, the values of degeneration, in the very seat of Christianity itself, — and even in the hearts of those sitting there, — Luther, that cursed monk, not only restored the Church, but, what was a thousand times worse, restored Christianity, and at a time too when it lay defeated. Christianity, the *Denial of the Will to Live*, exalted to a religion ! Luther was an impossible monk who, thanks to his own "impossibility," attacked the Church, and in so doing restored it ! Catholics would be perfectly justified in celebrating feasts in honour of Luther, and in producing festival plays in his honour. Luther and the "rebirth of morality" ! May all psychology go to the devil ! Without a shadow of a doubt the Germans are idealists. On two occasions when, at the cost of enormous courage and self-control, an upright, unequivocal, and perfectly scientific attitude of mind had been attained, the Germans were able to discover back stairs leading down to the old "ideal" again, compromises between truth and the "ideal," and,

in short, formulæ for the right to reject science and
to perpetrate falsehoods. Leibniz and Kant — these
two great breaks upon the intellectual honesty of
Europe ! Finally, at a moment when there appeared on the bridge that spanned two centuries of
decadence, a superior force of genius and will which
was strong enough to consolidate Europe and to
convert it into a political and economic unit, with
the object of ruling the world, the Germans, with
their Wars of Independence, robbed Europe of the
significance — the marvellous significance, of Napoleon's life. And in so doing they laid on their conscience everything that followed, everything that
exists today, — this sickliness and want of reason
which is most opposed to culture, and which is called
Nationalism, — this *névrose nationale* from which
Europe is suffering acutely ; this eternal subdivision
of Europe into petty states, with politics on a muni-
cipal scale : they have robbed Europe itself of its
significance, of its reason, — and have stuffed it into
a cul-de-sac. Is there anyone except me who
knows the way out of this cul-de-sac ? Does anyone except me know of an aspiration which would
be great enough to bind the people of Europe once
more together ?

* * *

3

THE GENEALOGY OF MORALS

The revolt of the slaves in morals begins in the very principle of resentment becoming creative and giving birth to values — a resentment experienced by creatures who, deprived as they are of the proper outlet of action, are forced to find their compensation in an imaginary revenge. While every aristocratic morality springs from a triumphant affirmation of its own demands, the slave morality says "no" from the very outset to what is "outside itself," "different from itself," and "not itself" : and this "no" is its creative deed. This volte-face of the valuing standpoint — this inevitable gravitation to the objective instead of back to the subjective — is typical of "resentment" : the *slave-morality* requires as the condition of its existence an external and objective world, to employ physiological terminology, it requires objective stimuli to be capable of action at all — its action is fundamentally a reaction. The contrary is the case when we come to the aristocrat's system of values : it acts and grows spontaneously, it merely seeks its antithesis in order to pronounce a more grateful and exultant "yes" to its own self ; — its negative conception, "low," "vulgar," "bad," is merely a pale late-born foil in comparison with its positive and fundamental conception (saturated as it is with life and passion), of "we aristocrats, we good ones, we beautiful ones, we happy ones."

When the aristocratic morality goes astray and commits sacrilege on reality, this is limited to that particular sphere with which it is not sufficiently acquainted — a sphere, in fact, from the real knowl-

edge of which it disdainfully defends itself. It mis-
judges, in some cases, the sphere which it despises,
the sphere of the common vulgar man and the low
people : on the other hand, due weight should be
given to the consideration that in any case the mood
of contempt, of disdain, of superciliousness, even
on the supposition that it falsely portrays the object
of its contempt, will always be far removed from
that degree of falsity which will always characterise
the attacks — in effigy, of course — of the vindictive
hatred and revengefulness of the weak in onslaughts
on their enemies. In point of fact, there is in contempt too strong an admixture of nonchalance, of
casualness, of boredom, of impatience, even of personal exultation, for it to be capable of distorting
its victim into a real caricature or a real monstrosity.
Attention again should be paid to the almost benevo-
lent nuances which, for instance, the Greek nobility
imports into all the words by which it distinguishes
the common people from itself ; note how continu-
ously a kind of pity, care, and consideration imparts
its honeyed flavour, until at last almost all the words
which are applied to the vulgar man survive finally
as expressions for "unhappy," "worthy of pity"
(compare δειλός, δείλαιος, πονηρός, μοχθηρός ; the latter
two names really denoting the vulgar man as labour-
slave and beast of burden) — and how, conversely,
"bad," "low," "unhappy" have never ceased to ring
in the Greek ear with a tone in which "unhappy"
is the predominant note : this is a heritage of the old
noble aristocratic morality, which remains true to
itself even in contempt (let philologists remember
the sense in which ὀϊζυρός, ἄνολβος, τλήμων, δυστυχεῖν,
ξυμφορά used to be employed. The "well-born"

simply *felt* themselves the "happy"; they did not have to manufacture their happiness artificially through looking at their enemies, or in cases to talk and lie themselves into happiness (as is the custom with all resentful men); and similarly, complete men as they were, exuberant with strength, and consequently necessarily energetic, they were too wise to dissociate happiness from action — activity becomes in their minds necessarily counted as happiness (that is the etymology of εὖ πράττειν) — all in sharp contrast to the "happiness" of the weak and the oppressed, with their festering venom and malignity, among whom happiness appears essentially as a narcotic, a deadening, a quietude, a peace, a "Sabbath," an enervation of the mind and relaxation of the limbs, — in short, a purely passive phenomenon. While the aristocratic man lived in confidence and openness with himself (γενναῖος, "noble-born," emphasises the nuance "sincere," and perhaps also "naïf"), the resentful man, on the other hand, is neither sincere nor naïf, nor honest and candid with himself. His soul *squints*; his mind loves hidden crannies, tortuous paths and back-doors, everything secret appeals to him as *his* world, *his* safety, *his* balm; he is past master in silence, in not forgetting, in waiting, in provisional self-depreciation and self-abasement. A race of such resentful men will of necessity eventually prove more prudent than any aristocratic race, it will honour prudence on quite a distinct scale, as, in fact, a paramount condition of existence, while prudence among aristocratic men is apt to be tinged with a delicate flavour of luxury and refinement; so among them it plays nothing like so integral a part as that complete certainty of function of the governing *unconscious* instincts, or as indeed a certain lack of prudence, such as a vehement and valiant charge, whether against danger or the enemy, or as those ecstatic bursts of rage, love, reverence, gratitude, by which at all times noble souls have recognised each other. When the resentment of the aristocratic man manifests itself, it fulfils and exhausts itself in an immediate reaction, and consequently instills no venom : on the other hand, it never manifests itself at all in countless instances, when in the case of the feeble and weak it would be inevitable. An inability to take seriously for any length of time their enemies, their disasters, their misdeeds — that is the sign of the full strong natures who possess a superfluity of moulding plastic force, that heals completely and produces forgetfulness : a good example of this in the modern world is Mirabeau, who had no memory for any insults and meannesses which were practised on him, and who was only incapable of forgiving because he forgot. Such a man indeed shakes off with a shrug many a worm which would have buried itself in another ; it is only in characters like these that we see the possibility (supposing, of course, that there is such a possibility in the world) of the real "love of one's enemies." What respect for his enemies is found, forsooth, in an aristocratic man — and such a reverence is already a bridge to love ! He insists on having his enemy to himself as his distinction. He tolerates no other enemy but a man in whose character there is nothing to despise and much to honour ! On the other hand, imagine the "enemy" as the resentful man conceives him — and it is here exactly that we see his work, his creativeness ; he has conceived "the evil enemy," the "evil one," and indeed that is the root idea from which he now evolves as a contrasting and corresponding figure a "good one," himself — his very self !

*   *   *

4

EUROPEAN NIHILISM

Concerning great things one should either be silent or one should speak loftily : — loftily — that is to say, cynically and innocently.

What I am now going to relate is the history of the next two centuries. I shall describe what will happen, what must necessarily happen : *the triumph of Nihilism.* This history can be written already ; for necessity itself is at work in bringing it about. This future is already proclaimed by a hundred different omens ; as a destiny it announces its advent everywhere ; for this music of tomorrow all ears are already pricked. The whole of our culture in Europe has long been writhing in an agony of suspense which increases from decade to decade as if in expectation of a catastrophe : restless, violent, helter-skelter, like a torrent that will reach its bourne, and refuses to reflect — yea, that even dreads reflection.

On the other hand, the present writer has done little else, hitherto, than reflect and meditate, like an instinctive philosopher and anchorite, who found his advantage in isolation — in remaining outside, in patience, procrastination, and lagging behind ; like a weighing and testing spirit who has already lost his way in every labyrinth of the future ; like a prophetic bird-spirit that looks backwards when it would announce what is to come ; like the first perfect European Nihilist, who, however, has already outlived Nihilism in his own soul — who has outgrown, overcome, and dismissed it.

For the reader must not misunderstand the meaning of the title which has been given to this Evangel of the Future.*   With this formula a counter-movement finds expression, in regard to both a principle and a mission ; a movement which in some remote future will supersede this perfect Nihilism ; but which nevertheless regards it as a necessary step, both logically and psychologically, towards its own advent, and which positively cannot come, except on top of and out of it. For, why is the triumph of Nihilism inevitable now ? Because the very values current amongst us today will arrive at their logical conclusion in Nihilism, — because Nihilism is the only possible outcome of our greatest values and ideals, — because we must first experience Nihilism before we can realise what the actual worth of these "values" was. . . Sooner or later we shall be in need of *new values.*

* *The Will to Power: An Attempted Transvaluation of all Values.*

Nihilism is at our door : whence comes this most gruesome of all guests to us ? — To begin with, it is a mistake to point to "social evils," "physiological degeneration," or even to corruption as a cause of Nihilism. This is the most straightforward and most sympathetic age that ever was. Evil, whether spiritual, physical, or intellectual, is, in itself, quite unable to introduce Nihilism, i.e., the absolute repudiation of worth, purpose, desirability. These evils allow of yet other and quite different explanations. But there is one very definite explanation of the phenomena : Nihilism harbours in the heart of Christian morals.

The downfall of Christianity, — through its morality (which is insuperable), which finally turns against the Christian God Himself (the sense of truth, highly developed through Christianity, ultimately revolts against the falsehood and fictiousness of all Christian interpretations of the world and its history. The recoil-stroke of "God is Truth" in the fanatical Belief, is : "All is false." Buddhism of *action*. . .)

Doubt in morality is the decisive factor. The downfall of the moral interpretation of the universe, which loses its *raison d'être* once it has tried to take flight to a Beyond, meets its end in Nihilism. "Nothing has any purpose" (the inconsistency of one explanation of the world, to which men have devoted untold energy, — gives rise to the suspicion that all explanations may perhaps be false). The Buddhistic feature : a yearning for nonentity (Indian Buddhism has no fundamentally moral development at the back of it ; that is why Nihilism in its case means only morality not overcome ; existence is regarded as a punishment and conceived as an error ; error is thus held to be punishment — a moral valuation). Philosophical attempts to overcome the "moral God" (Hegel, Pantheism). The vanquishing of popular ideals : the wizard, the saint, the bard. Antagonism of "true" and "beautiful" and "good."

Against "purposelessness" on the one hand, against moral valuations on the other : how far has all science and philosophy been cultivated heretofore under the influence of moral judgments ? And have we not got the additional factor — the enmity of science, into the bargain ? Or the prejudice against science ? Criticism of Spinoza. Christian valuations everywhere present as remnants in socialistic and positivistic systems. A criticism of Christian morality is altogether lacking.

The Nihilistic consequences of present natural science (along with its attempts to escape into a Beyond). Out of its practice there finally *arises* a certain self-annihilation, an antagonistic attitude towards itself — a sort of anti-scientificality. Since Copernicus man has been rolling away from the centre towards *x*.

The Nihilistic consequences of the political and politico-economical way of thinking, where all principles at length become tainted with the atmosphere of the platform : the breath of mediocrity, insignificance, dishonesty, etc. Nationalism. Anarchy, etc. Punishment. Everywhere the deliverer is missing, either as a class or as a single man — the justifier.

Nihilistic consequences of history and of the "practical historian," i.e., the romanticist. The attitude of art is quite unoriginal in modern life. Its gloominess. Goethe's so-called Olympian State.

Art and the preparation of Nihilism. Romanticism (the conclusion of Wagner's *Ring of the Nibelung*).

What does Nihilism mean ? — That the highest values are losing their value. There is no bourne. There is no answer to the question : "to what purpose ?"

Thorough Nihilism is the conviction that life is absurd, in the light of the highest values already discovered ; it also includes the view that we have not the smallest right to assume the existence of transcendental objects or things in themselves, which would be either divine or morality incarnate.

This view is a result of fully developed "truthfulness" : therefore a consequence of the belief in morality.

What advantages did the Christian hypothesis of morality offer ?

(1) It bestowed an intrinsic value upon men, which contrasted with their apparent insignificance and subordination to chance in the eternal flux of becoming and perishing.

(2) It served the purpose of God's advocates, inasmuch as it granted the world a certain perfection despite its sorrow and evil — it also granted the world that proverbial "freedom" : evil seemed full of meaning.

(3) It assumed that man could have a knowledge of absolute values, and thus granted him adequate perception for the most important things.

(4) It prevented man from despising himself as man, from turning against life, and from being driven to despair by knowledge : it was a self-preservative measure.

In short : Morality was the great antidote against practical and theoretical Nihilism.

Nihilism will have to manifest itself as a *psychological condition*, first when we have sought in all that has happened a purpose which is not there : so that the seeker will ultimately lose courage. Nihilism is therefore the coming into consciousness of the long waste of strength, the pain of "futility," uncertainty, the lack of an opportunity to recover in some way, or to attain to a state of peace concerning anything — shame in one's own presence, as if one had cheated oneself too long. . . The purpose above-mentioned might have been achieved : in the form of a "realisation" of a most high canon of morality in all worldly phenomena, the moral order of the universe ; or in the form of the increase of love and harmony in the traffic of humanity ; or in the nearer approach to a general condition of happiness ; or even in the march towards general nonentity — any sort of goal always constitutes a purpose. The common factor to all these appearances is that something will be *attained*, through the process itself : and now we perceive that Becoming has been aiming at nothing, and has achieved nothing. Hence the disillusionment in regard to a so-called purpose in existence, as a cause of Nihilism ; whether this be in respect of a very definite purpose, or generalised into the recognition that all the hypotheses are false which have hitherto been offered as to the object of life, and which relate to the whole of "Evolution" (man no longer an assistant in, let alone the culmination of, the evolutionary process).

Nihilism will manifest itself as a psychological condition, in the second place, when man has fixed a totality, a systematisation, even an organisation in and behind all phenomena, so that the soul thirsting for respect and admiration will wallow in the general idea of a highest ruling and administrative power (if it be the soul of a logician, the sequence of consequences and perfect reasoning will suffice to conciliate everything). A kind of unity, some form of "monism" : and as a result of this belief man becomes obsessed by a feeling of profound relativity and dependence in the presence of an All which is infinitely superior to him, a sort of divinity. "The general good exacts the surrender of the individual . . ." but lo, there is no such general good ! At bottom, man loses the belief in his own worth

when no infinitely precious entity manifests itself
through him — that is to say, he conceived such an
All, *in order to be able to believe in his own worth.*

Nihilism, as a psychological condition, has yet a
third and last form. Admitting these two points
of view : that no purpose can be assigned to Becoming, and that no great entity rules behind all
Becoming, in which the individual may completely
lose himself as in an element of superior value ;
there still remains the subterfuge which would consist in condemning this whole world of Becoming
as an illusion, and in discovering a world which
would lie beyond it, and would be a real world.
The moment, however, that man perceives that
this world has been devised only for the purpose
of meeting certain psychological needs, and that
he has no right whatsoever to it, the final form of
Nihilism comes into being, which comprises a denial
of a metaphysical world, and which forbids itself
all belief in a real world. From this standpoint, the
reality of Becoming is the only reality that is admitted : all bypaths to back-worlds and false god-
heads are abandoned — but *this world is no longer
endured, although no one wishes to disown it.*

What has actually happened ? The feeling of
worthlessness was realised when it was understood
that neither the notion of "Purpose," nor that of
"Unity," nor that of "Truth," could be made to
interpret the general character of existence. Nothing is achieved or obtained thereby ; the unity which
intervenes in the multiplicity of events is entirely
lacking : the character of existence is not "true," it
is false ; there is certainly no longer any reason to
believe in a real world. In short, the categories,

"Purpose," "Unity," "Being," by means of which
we had lent some worth to life, we have once more
divorced from it — and the world now appears
worthless to us. . .

Nihilism. It may be two things : —
A. Nihilism as a sign of enhanced spiritual
strength : active Nihilism.
B. Nihilism as a sign of the collapse and decline
of spiritual strength : passive Nihilism.

Nihilism, a normal condition.
It may be a sign of strength ; spiritual vigour may
have increased to such an extent that the goals
toward which man has marched hitherto (the "convictions," articles of faith) are no longer suited to
it (for a faith generally expresses the exigencies of
the conditions of existence, a submission to the authority of an order of things which conduces to the
prosperity, the growth and power of a living creature . . .) ; on the other hand, a sign of insufficient
strength, to fix a goal, a "wherefore," and a faith for
itself.
It reaches its maximum of relative strength, as
a powerful destructive force, in the form of *active*
Nihilism.
Its opposite would be *weary* Nihilism, which no
longer attacks : its most renowned form being Buddhism : as *passive* Nihilism, a sign of weakness :
spiritual strength may be fatigued, exhausted, so
that the goals and values which have prevailed
hitherto are no longer suited to it and are no longer

believed in — so that the synthesis of values and
goals (upon which every strong culture stands) de-
composes, and the different values contend with
one another : Disintegration, then everything which
is relieving, which heals, becalms, or stupefies, steps
into the foreground under the cover of various dis-
guises, either religious, moral, political or æsthetic,
etc.

The time is coming when we shall have to pay
for having been Christians for two thousand years :
we are losing the firm footing which enabled us to
live — for a long while we shall not know in what
direction we are travelling. We are hurling ourselves headlong into the opposite valuations, with
that degree of energy which could only have been
engendered in man by an overvaluation of himself.

Now, everything is false from the root, words
and nothing but words, confused, feeble, or over-
strained.

(a) There is a seeking after a sort of earthly
solution of the problem of life, but in the same sense
as that of the *final triumph* of truth, love, justice
(socialism : "equality of persons").

(b) There is also an attempt to hold fast to the
moral ideal (with altruism, self-sacrifice, and the
denial of the will, in the front rank).

(c) There is even an attempt to hold fast to a
"Beyond" : were it only as an antilogical x ; but it
is forthwith interpreted in such a way that a kind
of metaphysical solace, after the old style, may be
derived from it.

(d) There is an attempt to read the phenomena
of life in such a way as to arrive at the divine
guidance of old, with its powers of rewarding,

punishing, educating, and of generally conducing to a something better in the order of things.

(e) People once more believe in good and evil ; so that the victory of the good and the annihilation of the evil is regarded as a duty (this is English, and is typical of that blockhead, John Stuart Mill).

(f) The contempt felt for "naturalness," for the desires and for the ego : the attempt to regard even the highest intellectuality and art as a result of an impersonal and disinterested attitude.

(g) The Church is still allowed to meddle in all the essential occurrences and incidents in the life of the individual, with a view to consecrating it and giving it a *loftier* meaning : we still have the "Christian State" and the "Christian marriage."

After thousands of years of error and confusion, it is my good fortune to have rediscovered the road which leads to a Yea and to a Nay.

I teach people to say Nay in the face of all that makes for weakness and exhaustion.

I teach people to say Yea in the face of all that makes for strength, that preserves strength, and justifies the feeling of strength.

Up to the present, neither the one nor the other has been taught ; but rather virtue, disinterestedness, pity, and even the negation of life. All these are values proceeding from exhausted people.

After having pondered over the physiology of exhaustion for some time, I was led to the question : to what extent the judgments of exhausted people had percolated into the world of values.

The result at which I arrived was as startling as it

could possibly be — even for one like myself who was already at home in many a strange world : I found that all prevailing values — that is to say, all those which had gained ascendancy over humanity, or at least over its tamer portions, could be traced back to the judgment of exhausted people.

Under the cover of the holiest names, I found the most destructive tendencies ; people had actually given the name "God" to all that renders weak, teaches weakness, and infects with weakness. . . I found that the "good man" was a form of self-affirmation on the part of decadence.

That virtue which Schopenhauer still proclaimed as superior to all, and as the most fundamental of all virtues ; even that same pity I recognised as more dangerous than any vice. Deliberately to thwart the law of selection among species, and their natural means of purging their stock of degenerate members — this, up to my time, had been the greatest of all virtues. . .

One should do honour to the fatality which says to the feeble : "perish !"

The opposing of this fatality, the botching of mankind and the allowing of it to putrefy, was given the name "God." One shall not take the name of the Lord one's God in vain. . .

The race is corrupted — not by its vices, but by its ignorance : it is corrupted becaues it has not recognised exhaustion as exhaustion : physiological misunderstandings are the cause of all evil.

Virtue is our greatest misunderstanding.

Problem : how were the exhausted able to make the laws of values ? In other words, how did they who are the last, come to power ? . . . How did the instincts of the animal man ever get to stand on their heads ? . . .

This perishing seems like self-annihilation, like an instinctive selection of that which must destroy. The symptoms of this self-destruction of the botched and the bungled : self-vivisection, poisoning, intoxication, romanticism, and, above all, the instinctive constraint to acts whereby the powerful are made into mortal enemies (training, so to speak, one's own hangmen), the will to destruction as the will of a still deeper instinct — of the instinct of self-destruction, of the Will to Nonentity.

What class of men will prove they are strongest in this new order of things ? The most moderate — they who do not require any extreme forms of belief, they who not only admit of, but actually like, a certain modicum of chance and nonsense ; they who can think of man with a very moderate view of his value, without becoming weak and small on that account ; the most rich in health, who are able to withstand a maximum amount of sorrow, and who are therefore not so very much afraid of sorrow — men who are certain of their power, and who represent with conscious pride the state of strength to which man has attained.

* * *

How could such a man think of Eternal Recurrence ?

The Periods of European Nihilism.

The Period of Obscurity : all kinds of groping measures devised to preserve old institutions and not to arrest the progress of new ones.

The Period of Light : men see that old and new are fundamental contraries ; that the old values are born of descending life, and that the new ones are born of ascending life — that *all old ideals* are unfriendly to life (born of decadence and determining it, however much they may be decked out in the Sunday finery of morality). We understand the old, but are far from being sufficiently strong for the new.

The Periods of the Three Great Passions : contempt, pity, destruction.

The Periods of Catastrophes : the rise of a teaching which will sift mankind . . . which drives the weak to some decision and the strong also.

The slow advance and rise of the middle and lower classes (including the lower kind of spirit and body), which was already well under way before the French Revolution, and would have made the same progress forward without the latter, — in short, then, the preponderance of the herd over all herdsmen and bell-wethers, — brings in its train : —

(1) Gloominess of spirit (the juxtaposition of a stoical and a frivolous appearance of happiness, peculiar to noble cultures, is on the decline ; much suffering is allowed to be seen and heard which formerly was borne in concealment ;

(2) Moral hypocrisy (a way of distinguishing

oneself through morality, but by means of the values of the herd : pity, solicitude, moderation ; and not by means of those virtues which are recognised and honoured outside the herd's sphere of power) ;

(3) A really large amount of sympathy with both pain and joy (a feeling of pleasure resulting from being herded together, which is peculiar to all gregarious animals — "public spirit," "patriotism," everything, in fact, which is apart from the individual).

Why does everything become mummery. — The modern man is lacking in unfailing instinct (instinct being understood here to mean that which is the outcome of a long period of activity in the same occupation on the part of one family of men) ; the incapability of producing anything perfect, is simply the result of this lack of instinct : one individual alone cannot make up for the schooling his ancestors should have transmitted to him.

What a morality or book of law creates : that deep instinct which renders automatism and perfection possible in life and in work.

But now we have reached the opposite point ; yes, we wanted to reach it — the most extreme consciousness, through introspection on the part of man and of history : and thus we are practically most distant from perfection in Being, doing, and willing : our desires — even our will to knowledge — shows how prodigiously decadent we are. We are striving after the very reverse of what *strong races* and *strong natures* will have — understanding is an *end.* . .

The Three Centuries.

Their different kinds of sensitiveness may perhaps be best expressed as follows : —

Aristocracy : Descartes, the reign of *reason*, evidence showing the sovereignty of the *will*.

Feminism : Rousseau, the reign of *feeling*, evidence showing the sovereignty of the senses ; all lies.

Animalism : Schopenhauer, the reign of *passion*, evidence showing the sovereignty of animality, more honest, but gloomy.

The seventeenth century is *aristocratic*, all for order, haughty towards everything animal, severe in regard to the heart, "austere," and even free from sentiment, "non-German," averse to all that is burlesque and natural, generalising and maintaining an attitude of sovereignty towards the past : for it believes in itself. At bottom it partakes very much of the beast of prey, and practises asceticism in order to remain master. It is the century of strength of will, as also that of strong passion.

The eighteenth century is dominated by *woman*, it is gushing, spiritual, and flat ; but with intellect at the service of aspirations and of the heart, it is a libertine in the pleasures of intellect, undermining all authorities ; emotionally intoxicated, cheerful, clear, humane, and sociable, false to itself and at bottom very rascally. . .

The nineteenth century is more *animal*, more subterranean, hateful, realistic, plebeian, and on that very account "better," "more honest," more submissive to "reality" of what kind soever, and truer ; but weak of will, sad, obscurely exacting and fatalistic. It has no feeling of timidity or reverence, either in the presence of "reason" or the "heart" ; thoroughly convinced of the dominion of the desires (Schopenhauer said "Will," but nothing is more characteristic of his philosophy than that it entirely lacks all actual willing). Even morality is reduced to an instinct ("Pity").

Auguste Comte is the continuation of the eighteenth century (the dominion of the heart over the head, sensuality in the theory of knowledge, altruistic exaltation).

The fact that science has become as sovereign as it is today, proves how the nineteenth century has emancipated itself from the dominion of ideals. A certain absence of "needs" and wishes makes our scientific curiosity and rigour possible — this is our kind of virtue.

Romanticism is the counterstroke of the eighteenth century ; a sort of accumulated longing for its grand style of exaltation (as a matter of fact, largely mingled with mummery and self-deception : the desire was to represent strong nature and strong passion).

Against Rousseau. — Alas ! man is no longer sufficiently evil ; Rousseau's opponents, who say that "man is a beast of prey," are unfortunately wrong. Not the corruption of man, but the softening and moralising of him is the curse. In the sphere which Rousseau attacked most violently, the relatively strongest and most successful type of man was still to be found (the type which still possessed the great passions intact : Will to Power, Will to Pleasure, the Will and Ability to Command). The man of the eighteenth century must be compared with the man of the Renaissance (also with the man of the seventeenth century in France) if the matter is to be understood at all : Rousseau is a symptom of self-contempt and of inflamed vanity — both signs that the dominating will is lacking : he moralises and seeks the cause of his own misery after the style of a revengeful man in the *ruling* classes.

The advance of the nineteenth century upon the eighteenth (at bottom we good Europeans are carrying on a war against the eighteenth century) :

(1) "The return to Nature" is getting to be understood, ever more definitely, in a way which is quite the reverse of that in which Rousseau used the phrase — *away from idylls and operas !*

(2) Ever more decided, more anti-idealistic, more objective, more fearless, more industrious, more temperate, more suspicious of sudden changes, *anti-revolutionary ;*

(3) The question of bodily health is being pressed ever more decidedly in front of the health of "the soul" : the latter is regarded as a condition brought about by the former, and bodily health is believed to be, at least, the prerequisite to spiritual health.

It is the time of the great noon, of the most appalling enlightenment : my particular kind of Pessimism : the great starting-point.

(1) Fundamental contradiction between civilisation and the elevation of man.

(2) Moral valuations regarded as a history of lies

and the art of calumny in the service of the Will to Power (of the will of the herd, which rises against stronger men).

(3) The conditions which determine every eleva- tion in culture (the facilitation of a selection being made at the cost of a crowd) are the conditions of all growth.

(4) The multiformity of the world as a question of *strength*, which sees all things in the perspective of their growth. The moral Christian values to be regarded as the insurrection and mendacity of slaves (in comparison with the aristocratic values of the ancient world).

* * *

III

THE WORLD WITHOUT GOD

I

THE BIRTH OF TRAGEDY OUT OF THE SPIRIT OF MUSIC

We shall have gained much for the science of æsthetics, when once we have perceived not only by logical inference, but by the immediate certainty of intuition, that the continuous development of art is bound up with the duplexity of the *Apollonian* and the *Dionysian* : in like manner as procreation is dependent on the duality of the sexes, involving perpetual conflicts with only periodically interven-

ing reconciliations. These names we borrow from
the Greeks, who disclose to the intelligent observer
the profound mysteries of their view of art, not
indeed in concepts, but in the impressively clear
figures of their world of deities. It is in connection with Apollo and Dionysus, the two art-deities
of the Greeks, that we learn that there existed in
the Grecian world a wide antithesis, in origin and
aims, between the art of the shaper, the Apollonian,
and the non-plastic art of music, that of Dionysus :
both these so heterogeneous tendencies run parallel
to each other, for the most part openly at variance,
and continually inciting each other to new and more
powerful births, to perpetuate in them the strife of
this antithesis, which is but seemingly bridged over
by their mutual term "Art" ; till at last, by a metaphysical miracle of the Hellenic will, they appear
paired with each other, and through this pairing
eventually generate the equally Dionysian and Apollonian art-work of Attic tragedy.

From all quarters of the Ancient World — to say
nothing of the modern — from Rome as far as Baby-
lon, we can prove the existence of Dionysian festivals, the type of which bears, at best, the same relation to the Greek festivals as the bearded satyr,
who borrowed his name and attributes from the
goat, does to Dionysus himself. In nearly every
instance the centre of these festivals lay in extravagant sexual licentiousness, the waves of which overwhelmed all family life and its venerable traditions ;
the very wildest beasts of nature were let loose here,
including that detestable mixture of lust and cruelty
which has always seemed to me the genuine "witches'
draught." For some time, however, it would seem

that the Greeks were perfectly secure and guarded against the feverish agitations of these festivals (— the knowledge of which entered Greece by all the channels of land and sea) by the figure of Apollo himself rising here in full pride, who could not have held out the Gorgon's head to a more dangerous power than this grotesquely uncouth Dionysian. It is in Doric art that this majestically-rejecting attitude of Apollo perpetuated itself. This opposition became more precarious and even impossible, when, from out of the deepest root of the Hellenic nature, similar impulses finally broke forth and made way for themselves : the Delphic god, by a seasonably effected reconciliation, was now contented with taking the destructive arms from the hands of his powerful antagonist. This reconciliation marks the most important moment in the history of the Greek cult : wherever we turn our eyes we may observe the revolutions resulting from this event. It was the reconciliation of two antagonists, with the sharp demarcation of the boundary-lines to be thenceforth observed by each, and with periodical transmission of testimonials ; — in reality, the chasm was not bridged over. But if we observe how, under the pressure of this conclusion of peace, the Dionysian power manifested itself, we shall now recognise in the Dionysian orgies of the Greeks, as compared with the Babylonian Sacæa and their retrogression of man to the tiger and the ape, the significance of festivals of world-redemption and days of transfiguration. Not till then does nature attain her artistic jubilee ; not till then does the rupture of the *principium individuationis* become an artistic phenomenon. That horrible "witches'

draught" of sensuality and cruelty was here power-
less : only the curious blending and duality in the
emotions of the Dionysian revellers reminds one of
it — just as medicines remind one of deadly poisons,
— that phenomenon, to wit, that pains beget joy,
that jubilation wrings painful sounds out of the
breast. From the highest joy sounds the cry of
horror or the yearning wail over an irretrievable
loss. In these Greek festivals a sentimental trait,
as it were, breaks forth from nature, as if she must
sigh over her dismemberment into individuals. The
song and pantomime of such dually-minded revellers was something new and unheard-of in the
Homeric-Grecian world : and the Dionysian music
in particular excited awe and horror. If music, as
it would seem, was previously known as an Apollonian art, it was, strictly speaking, only as the wave-
beat of rhythm, the formative power of which was
developed to the representation of Apollonian conditions. The music of Apollo was Doric archi-
tectonics in tones, but in merely suggested tones,
such as those of the cithara. The very element
which forms the essence of Dionysian music (and
hence of music in general) is carefully excluded as
un-Apollonian ; namely, the thrilling power of the
tone, the uniform stream of the melos, and the thoroughly incomparable world of harmony. In the
Dionysian dithyramb man is incited to the highest
exaltation of all his symbolic faculties ; something
never before experienced struggles for utterance —
the annihilation of the veil of Mâyâ, Oneness as
genius of the race, ay, of nature. The essence of
nature is now to be expressed symbolically ; a new

world of symbols is required ; for once the entire
symbolism of the body, not only the symbolism of
the lips, face, and speech, but the whole pantomime
of dancing which sets all the members into rhythmi-
cal motion. Thereupon the other symbolic powers,
those of music, in rhythmics, dynamics, and harmony, suddenly become impetuous. To comprehend this collective discharge of all the symbolic
powers, a man must have already attained that height
of self-abnegation, which wills to express itself symbolically through these powers : the Dithyrambic
votary of Dionysus is therefore understood only by
those like himself ! With what astonishment must
the Apollonian Greek have beheld him ! With an
astonishment, which was all the greater the more
it was mingled with the shuddering suspicion that
all this was in reality not so very foreign to him,
yea, that, like unto a veil, his Apollonian consciousness only hid this Dionysian world from his view.

There is an ancient story that king Midas hunted
in the forest a long time for the wise Silenus, the
companion of Dionysus, without capturing him.
When at last he fell into his hands, the king asked
what was best of all and most desirable for man.
Fixed and immovable, the demon remained silent ;
till at last, forced by the king, he broke out with
shrill laughter into these words : "Oh, wretched
race of a day, children of chance and misery, why
do ye compel me to say to you what it were most
expedient for you not to hear ? What is best of
all is for ever beyond your reach : not to be born,
not to be, to be nothing. The second best for you,
however, is soon to die."

How is the Olympian world of deities related to
this folk-wisdom? Even as the rapturous vision
of the tortured martyr to his sufferings.

Now the Olympian magic mountain opens, as it
were, to our view and shows to us its roots. The
Greek knew and felt the terrors and horrors of
existence : to be able to live at all, he had to inter-
pose the shining dream-birth of the Olympian world
between himself and them. The excessive distrust
of the titanic powers of nature, the Moira throning
inexorably over all knowledge, the vulture of the
great philanthropist Prometheus, the terrible fate of
the wise Œdipus, the family curse of the Atridæ
which drove Orestes to matricide ; in short, that
entire philosophy of the sylvan god, with its mythi-
cal exemplars, which wrought the ruin of the melancholy Etruscans — was again and again surmounted
anew by the Greeks through the artistic middle
world of the Olympians, or at least veiled and with-
drawn from sight. To be able to live, the Greeks
had, from direst necessity, to create these gods :
which process we may perhaps picture to ourselves
in this manner : that out of the original Titan
thearchy of terror the Olympian thearchy of
joy was evolved, by slow transitions, through the
Apollonian impulse to beauty, even as roses break
forth from thorny bushes. How else could this
so sensitive people, so vehement in its desires, so
singularly qualified for suffering, have endured existence, if it had not been exhibited to them in their
gods, surrounded with a higher glory ? The same
impulse which calls art into being, as the complement and consummation of existence, seducing to
a continuation of life, caused also the Olympian

world to arise, in which the Hellenic "will" held up before itself a transfiguring mirror.

We shall now have to avail ourselves of all the principles of art hitherto considered, in order to find our way through the labyrinth, as we must designate the origin of Greek tragedy. I shall not be charged with absurdity in saying that the problem of this origin has as yet not even been seriously stated, not to say solved, however often the fluttering tatters of ancient tradition have been sewed together in sundry combinations and torn asunder again. This tradition tells us in the most unequivocal terms, *that tragedy sprang from the tragic chorus*, and was originally only chorus and nothing but chorus : and hence we feel it our duty to look into the heart of this tragic chorus as being the real proto-drama, without in the least contenting ourselves with current art-phraseology — according to which the chorus is the ideal spectator, or represents the people in contrast to the regal side of the scene.

It is indeed an "ideal" domain, as Schiller rightly perceived, upon which the Greek satyric chorus, the chorus of primitive tragedy, was wont to walk, a domain raised far above the actual path of mortals. The Greek framed for this chorus the suspended scaffolding of a fictitious natural *state* and placed thereon fictitious natural *beings*. It is on this foundation that tragedy grew up, and so it could of course dispense from the very first with a painful portrayal of reality. Yet it is not an arbitrary world placed by fancy betwixt heaven and earth ; rather is it a world possessing the same reality and trustworthiness that Olympus with its dwellers possessed for the believing Hellene. The satyr, as being the

Dionysian chorist, lives in a religiously acknowledged reality under the sanction of the myth and
cult. That tragedy begins with him, that the Dionysian wisdom of tragedy speaks through him, is
just as surprising a phenomenon to us as, in general,
the derivation of tragedy from the chorus. Perhaps
we shall get a starting-point for our inquiry, if I put
forward the proposition that the satyr, the fictitious
natural being, is to the man of culture what Dionysian music is to civilisation. Concerning this
latter, Richard Wagner says that it is neutralised by
music even as lamplight by daylight. In like manner, I believe, the Greek man of culture felt himself neutralised in the presence of the satyric chorus :
and this is the most immediate effect of the Dionysian tragedy, that the state and society, and, in
general, the gaps between man and man give way
to an overwhelming feeling of oneness, which leads
back to the heart of nature. The metaphysical
comfort, — with which, as I have here intimated,
every true tragedy dismisses us — that, in spite of
the perpetual change of phenomena, life at bottom
is indestructibly powerful and pleasurable, this comfort appears with corporeal lucidity as the satyric
chorus, as the chorus of natural beings, who live
ineradicable as it were behind all civilisation, and
who, in spite of the ceaseless change of generations
and the history of nations, remain for ever the same.

With this chorus the deep-minded Hellene, who
is so singularly qualified for the most delicate and
severe suffering, consoles himself : — he who has
glanced with piercing eye into the very heart of the
terrible destructive processes of so-called universal
history, as also into the cruelty of nature, and is in

danger of longing for a Buddhistic negation of the will. Art saves him, and through art life saves him - for herself.

Owing to our learned conception of the elementary artistic processes, this artistic proto-phenomenon, which is here introduced to explain the tragic chorus, is almost shocking : while nothing can be more certain than that the poet is a poet only in that he beholds himself surrounded by forms which live and act before him, into the innermost being of which his glance penetrates. By reason of a strange defeat in our capacities, we modern men are apt to represent to ourselves the æsthetic proto-phenomenon as too complex and abstract. For the true poet the metaphor is not a rhetorical figure, but a vicarious image which actually hovers before him in place of a concept. The character is not for him an aggregate composed of a studied collection of particular traits, but an irrepressibly live person appearing before his eyes, and differing only from the corresponding vision of the painter by its ever continued life and action. Why is it that Homer sketches much more vividly than all the other poets ? Because he contemplates much more. We talk so abstractly about poetry, because we are all wont to be bad poets. At bottom the æsthetic phenomenon is simple : let a man but have the faculty of perpetually seeing a lively play and of constantly living surrounded by hosts of spirits, then he is a poet : let him but feel the impulse to transform himself and to talk from out the bodies and souls of others, then he is a dramatist.

The Dionysian excitement is able to impart to a whole mass of men this artistic faculty of seeing

themselves surrounded by such a host of spirits,
with whom they know themselves to be inwardly
one. This function of the tragic chorus is the dra-
matic proto-phenomenon : to see one's self transformed before one's self, and then to act as if one
had really entered into another body, into another
character. This function stands at the beginning
of the development of the drama. Here we have
something different from the rhapsodist, who does
not blend with his pictures, but only sees them, like
the painter, with contemplative eye outside of him ;
here we actually have a surrender of the individual
by his entering into another nature. Moreover this
phenomenon appears in the form of an epidemic :
a whole throng feels itself metamorphosed in this
wise. Hence it is that the dithyramb is essentially
different from every other variety of the choric
song. The virgins, who with laurel twigs in their
hands solemnly proceed to the temple of Apollo and
sing a processional hymn, remain what they are and
retain their civic names : the dithyrambic chorus is
a chorus of transformed beings, whose civic past
and social rank are totally forgotten : they have become the timeless servants of their god that live aloof
from all the spheres of society. Every other variety
of the choric lyric of the Hellenes is but an enormous enhancement of the Apollonian unit-singer :
while in the dithyramb we have before us a community of unconscious actors, who mutually regard
themselves as transformed among one another.

This enchantment is the prerequisite of all dra-
matic art. In this enchantment the Dionysian reveller sees himself as a satyr, *and as satyr he in turn
beholds the god*, that is, in his transformation he sees

a new vision outside him as the Apollonian consummation of his state. With this new vision the drama is complete.

According to this view, we must understand Greek tragedy as the Dionysian chorus, which always disburdens itself anew in an Apollonian world of pictures. The choric parts, therefore, with which tragedy is interlaced, are in a manner the mother-womb of the entire so-called dialogue, that is, of the whole stage-world, of the drama proper. In several successive outbursts does this primordial basis of tragedy beam forth the vision of the drama, which is a dream-phenomenon throughout, and, as such, epic in character : on the other hand, however, as objectivation of a Dionysian state, it does not represent the Apollonian redemption in appearance, but, conversely, the dissolution of the individual and his unification with primordial existence. Accordingly, the drama is the Apollonian embodiment of Dionysian perceptions and influences, and is thereby separated from the epic as by an immense gap.

Whatever rises to the surface in the dialogue of the Apollonian part of Greek tragedy, appears simple, transparent, beautiful. In this sense the dialogue is a copy of the Hellene, whose nature reveals itself in the dance, because in the dance the greatest energy is merely potential, but betrays itself nevertheless in flexible and vivacious movements. The language of the Sophoclean heroes, for instance, surprises us by its Apollonian precision and clearness, so that we at once imagine we see into the innermost recesses of their being, and marvel not a little that the way to these recesses is so short. But if for the moment we disregard the character of the hero which rises to the surface and grows visible — and which at bottom is nothing but the light-picture cast on a dark wall, that is, appearance through and through, — if rather we enter into the myth which projects itself in these bright mirrorings, we shall of a sudden experience a phenomenon which bears a reverse relation to one familiar in optics. When, after a vigorous effort to gaze into the sun, we turn away blinded we have dark-coloured spots before our eyes as restoratives, so to speak ; while, on the contrary, those light-picture phenomena of the Sophoclean hero, — in short, the Apollonian of the mask, — are the necessary productions of a glance into the secret and terrible things of nature, as it were shining spots to heal the eye which dire night has seared. Only in this sense can we hope to be able to grasp the true meaning of the serious and significant notion of "Greek cheerfulness" ; while of course we encounter the misunderstood notion of this cheerfulness, as resulting from a state of unendangered comfort, on all the ways and paths of the present time.

It is an indisputable tradition that Greek tragedy in its earliest form had for its theme only the sufferings of Dionysus, and that for some time the only stage-hero therein was simply Dionysus himself. With the same confidence, however, we can maintain that not until Euripides did Dionysus cease to be the tragic hero, and that in fact all the celebrated figures of the Greek stage — Prometheus, Œdipus, etc. — are but masks of this original hero, Dionysus. The presence of a god behind all these masks is the one essential cause of the typical "ideality," so oft exciting wonder, of these celebrated figures. Some one, I know not whom, has maintained that all individuals are comic as individuals and are consequently un-tragic : from whence it might be inferred that the Greeks in general could not endure individuals on the tragic stage. And they really seem to have had these sentiments : as, in general, it is to be observed that the Platonic discrimination and valuation of the "idea" in contrast to the "eidolon," the image, is deeply rooted in the Hellenic being. Availing ourselves of Plato's terminology, however, we should have to speak of the tragic figures of the Hellenic stage somewhat as follows. The one truly real Dionysus appears in a multiplicity of forms, in the mask of a fighting hero and entangled, as it were, in the net of an individual will. As the visibly appearing god now talks and acts, he resembles an erring, striving, suffering individual : and that, in general, he appears with such epic precision and clearness, is due to the dream-reading Apollo, who reads to the chorus its Dionysian state through this symbolic appearance. In reality, however, this hero is the suffering Dionysus of the mysteries, a god experiencing in himself the sufferings of individuation, of whom wonderful myths tell that as a boy he was dismembered by the Titans and has been worshipped in this state as Zagreus : whereby is intimated that this dismemberment, the properly Dionysian suffering, is like a transformation into air, water, earth, and fire, that we must therefore regard the state of individuation as the source and primal cause of all suffering, as something objectionable in itself. From the smile of this Dionysus sprang the Olympian gods, from his tears sprang man. In his existence as a dismembered god, Dionysus has the dual nature of a cruel barbarised demon, and a mild pacific ruler. But the hope of the epopts looked for a new birth of Dionysus, which we have now to conceive of in anticipation as the end of individuation : it was for this coming third Dionysus that the stormy jubilation-hymns of the epopts resounded. And it is only this hope that sheds a ray of joy upon the features of a world torn asunder and shattered into individuals : as is symbolised in the myth by Demeter sunk in eternal sadness, who rejoices again only when told that she may once more give birth to Dionysus. In the views of things here given we already have all the elements of a profound and pessimistic contemplation of the world, and along with these we have the mystery doctrine of tragedy : the fundamental knowledge of the oneness of all existing things, the consideration of individuation as the primal cause of evil, and art as the joyous hope that the spell of individuation may be broken, as the augury of a restored oneness.

From the nature of art, as it is ordinarily conceived according to the single category of appearance and beauty, the tragic cannot be honestly deduced at all ; it is only through the spirit of music that we understand the joy in the annihilation of the individual. For in the particular examples of such annihilation only is the eternal phenomenon of Dionysian art made clear to us, which gives expression to the will in its omnipotence, as it were, behind the *principium individuationis*, the eternal life beyond all phenomena, and in spite of all annihilation. The metaphysical delight in the tragic

is a translation of the instinctively unconscious
Dionysian wisdom into the language of the scene :
the hero, the highest manifestation of the will, is
disavowed for our pleasure, because he is only
phenomenon, and because the eternal life of the will
is not affected by his annihilation. "We believe in
eternal life," tragedy exclaims ; while music is the
proximate idea of this life. Plastic art has an altogether different object : here Apollo vanquishes the
suffering of the individual by the radiant glorifica-
tion of the eternity of the phenomenon ; here beauty
triumphs over the suffering inherent in life ; pain
is in a manner surreptitiously obliterated from the
features of nature. In Dionysian art and its tragic
symbolism the same nature speaks to us with its
true undissembled voice : "Be as I am ! Amidst
the ceaseless change of phenomena the eternally
creative primordial mother, eternally impelling to
existence, self-satisfying eternally with this change
of phenomena !"

Dionysian art, too, seeks to convince us of the
eternal joy of existence : only we are to seek this
joy not in phenomena, but behind phenomena.
We are to perceive how all that comes into being
must be ready for a sorrowful end ; we are com-
pelled to look into the terrors of individual existence — yet we are not to become torpid : a metaphysical comfort tears us momentarily from the
bustle of the transforming figures. We are really
for brief moments Primordial Being itself, and feel
its indomitable desire for being and joy in existence ;
the struggle, the pain, the destruction of phenomena,
now appear to us as something necessary, considering the surplus of innumerable forms of existence

which throng and push one another into life, considering the exuberant fertility of the universal will. We are pierced by the maddening sting of these pains at the very moment when we have become, as it were, one with the immeasurable primordial joy in existence, and when we anticipate, in Dionysian ecstasy, the indestructibility and eternity of this joy. In spite of fear and pity, we are the happy living beings, not as individuals, but as the one living being, with whose procreative joy we are blended.

EPILOGUE

Ay, what is Dionysian ? — In this book may be found an answer, — a "knowing one" speaks here, the votary and disciple of his god. Perhaps I should now speak more guardedly and less eloquently of a psychological question so difficult as the origin of tragedy among the Greeks. A fundamental question is the relation of the Greek to pain, his degree of sensibility, — did this relation remain constant ? or did it veer about ? — the question, whether his ever-increasing longing for beauty, for festivals, gaieties, new cults, did really grow out of want, privation, melancholy, pain ? For suppose even this to be true — and Pericles (or Thucydides) intimates as much in the great Funeral Speech : — whence then the opposite longing, which appeared first in the order of time, the *longing for the ugly*, the good, resolute desire of the Old Hellene for pessimism, for tragic myth, for the picture of all that is terrible, evil, enigmatical, destructive, fatal at the basis of existence, — whence then must tragedy have sprung ? Perhaps from joy, from strength,

from exuberant health, from over-fullness. And
what then, physiologically speaking, is the meaning
of that madness, out of which comic as well as tragic
art has grown, the Dionysian madness? What?
perhaps madness is not necessarily the symptom of
degeneration, of decline, of belated culture? Perhaps there are — a question for alienists — neuroses
of health? of folk-youth and -youthfulness? What
does that synthesis of god and goat in the Satyr
point to? What self-experience, what "stress,"
made the Greek think of the Dionysian reveller and
primitive man as a satyr? And as regards the
origin of the tragic chorus : perhaps there were
endemic ecstasies in the eras when the Greek body
bloomed and the Greek soul brimmed over with
life? Visions and hallucinations, which took hold
of entire communities, entire cult-assemblies?
What if the Greeks in the very wealth of their
youth had the will to be tragic and were pessimists?
What if it was madness itself, to use a word of
Plato's, which brought the greatest blessings upon
Hellas? And what if, on the other hand and conversely, at the very time of their dissolution and
weakness, the Greeks became always more optimis-
tic, more superficial, more histrionic, also more ardent for logic and the logicising of the world, — consequently at the same time more "cheerful" and
more "scientific"? Ay, despite all "modern ideas"
and prejudices of the democratic taste, may not the
triumph of optimism, the common sense that has
gained the upper hand, the practical and theoretical
utilitarianism, like democracy itself, with which it
is synchronous — be symptomatic of declining vigour, of approaching age, of physiological weari-

ness ? And not at all — pessimism ? Was Epi-
curus an optimist — because a sufferer ? . . . We
see it is a whole bundle of weighty questions which
this book has taken upon itself, — let us not fail
to add its weightiest question ! Viewed through
the optics of life, what is the meaning of —
morality ? . . .

*   *   *

2

THE TRUE AND THE APPARENT WORLD

What our Cheerfulness Signifies. — The most important of more recent events — that "God is dead,"
that the belief in the Christian God has become unworthy of belief — already begins to cast its first
shadows over Europe. To the few at least whose
eye, whose suspecting glance, is strong enough and
subtle enough for this drama, some sun seems to
have set, some old, profound confidence seems to
have changed into doubt : our old world must seem
to them daily more darksome, distrustful, strange
and "old." In the main, however, one may say that
the event itself is far too great, too remote, too much
beyond most people's power of apprehension, for
one to suppose that so much as the report of it could
have reached them ; not to speak of many who already knew what had taken place, and what must
all collapse now that this belief had been under-
mined, — because so much was built upon it, so much
rested on it, and had become one with it : for example, our entire European morality. This lengthy,
vast and uninterrupted process of crumbling, destruction, ruin and overthrow which is now im-

minent : who has realised it sufficiently today to have to stand up as the teacher and herald of such a tremendous logic of terror, as the prophet of a period of gloom and eclipse, the like of which has probably never taken place on earth before ? . . . Even we, the born riddle-readers, who wait as it were on the mountains posted 'twixt today and to-morrow, and engirt by their contradiction, we, the firstlings and premature children of the coming century, into whose sight especially the shadows which must forthwith envelop Europe should already have come — how is it that even we, without genuine sympathy for this period of gloom, contemplate its advent without any personal solicitude or fear ? Are we still, perhaps, too much under the immediate effects of the event — and are these effects, especially as regards ourselves, perhaps the reverse of what was to be expected — not at all sad and depressing, but rather like a new and indescribable variety of light, happiness, relief, enlivenment, encouragement, and dawning day ? . . . In fact, we philosophers and "free spirits" feel ourselves irradiated as by a new dawn by the report that the "old God is dead" ; our hearts overflow with gratitude, astonishment, presentiment and expectation. At last the horizon seems open once more, granting even that it is not bright ; our ships can at last put out to sea in face of every danger ; every hazard is again permitted to the discerner ; the sea, our sea, again lies open before us ; perhaps never before did such an "open sea" exist.

* * *

How the "True World" Ultimately Became a Fable. —

1. The true world, attainable to the sage, the pious man and the man of virtue, — he lives in it, *he is it.*

> (The most ancient form of the idea was relatively clever, simple, convincing. It was a paraphrase of the proposition "I, Plato, am the truth.")

2. The true world which is unattainable for the moment, is promised to the sage, to the pious man and to the man of virtue ("to the sinner who repents").

> (Progress of the idea : it becomes more subtle, more insidious, more evasive, — *it becomes a woman*, it becomes Christian.)

3. The true world is unattainable, it cannot be proved, it cannot promise anything ; but even as a thought, alone, it is a comfort, an obligation, a command.

> (At bottom this is still the old sun ; but seen through mist and scepticism : the idea has become sublime, pale, northern, Königsbergian.*)

4. The true world — is it unattainable ? At all events it is unattained. And as unattained it is also unknown. Consequently it no longer comforts, nor saves, nor constrains : what could something unknown constrain us to ?

> (The grey of dawn. Reason stretches itself and yawns for the first time. The cockcrow of positivism.)

---

* The philosopher Kant was born in Königsberg (Germany).

5. The "true world" — an idea that no longer serves any purpose, that no longer constrains one to anything, — a useless idea that has become quite superfluous, consequently an exploded idea : let us abolish it !

> (Bright daylight ; breakfast ; the return of common sense and of cheerfulness ; Plato blushes for shame and all free-spirits kick up a shindy.)

6. We have suppressed the true world : what world survives ? the apparent world perhaps ? . . . Certainly not ! *In abolishing the true world we have also abolished the world of appearance !*

> (Noon ; the moment of the shortest shadows ; the end of the longest error ; mankind's zenith ; Incipit Zarathustra.)

3

ETERNAL RECURRENCE

The Heaviest Burden. — What if a demon crept after thee into thy loneliest loneliness some day or night, and said to thee : "This life, as thou livest it at present, and hast lived it, thou must live it once more, and also innumerable times ; and there will be nothing new in it, but every pain and every joy and every thought and every sigh, and all the unspeakably small and great in thy life must come to thee again, and all in the same series and sequence — and similarly this spider and this moonlight among the trees, and similarly this moment, and I myself. The eternal sand-glass of existence will ever be turned once more, and thou with it, thou speck of dust !" — Wouldst thou not throw thyself down and gnash thy teeth, and curse the demon that so spake ? Or hast thou once experienced a tremendous moment in which thou wouldst answer him : "Thou art a God, and never did I hear anything so divine !" If that thought acquired power over thee as thou art, it would transform thee, and perhaps crush thee ; the question with regard to all and everything : "Dost thou want this once more, and also for innumerable times ?" would lie as the heaviest burden upon thy activity ! Or, how wouldst thou have to become favourably inclined to thyself and to life, so as to long for nothing more ardently than for this last eternal sanctioning and sealing ?

*   *   *

You feel that you will have to bid farewell, perhaps very soon — and this feeling's sunset glows into your happiness. Take heed of this sign : it means that you love life and yourself, life, as it met and formed you, — and that you desire to perpetuate it. — *Non alia sed hæc vita sempiterna* !

But realise too ! — that transitoriness sings her brief song again and again and that, harkening to the first bars, one nearly dies from longing at the idea that it may have passed for ever.

Do not look for distant, unknown blessedness and blessing and grace, but live thus that you want to live again and in all eternity ! Each moment reminds us of our task.

Main tendencies : 1. By all means plant love for life, love for your own life ! Whatever you invent to this end — if, through it, you really multiply joy in your own life — the next one must allow, as

much as it may go against his taste, and thereby ac-
quire a new, great tolerance.

2. To be determined in your enmity against
everything and everyone that tries to cast suspicion
upon the worth of life ; that is, against the obscur-
antists, the malcontents and the grumblers. Forbid
them reproduction ! Yet your enmity must become in itself a means to pleasure ! That is, smile,
jest, destroy without inner bitterness ! That is our
struggle to the death.

This life — your eternal life !

* * *

In order to endure the thought of recurrence,
freedom from morality is necessary ; new means
against the fact *pain* (pain regarded as the instrument, as the father of pleasure ; there is no accretive
consciousness of pain) ; pleasure derived from all
kinds of uncertainty and tentativeness, as a counter-
poise to extreme fatalism ; suppression of the concept "necessity" ; suppression of the "will" ; suppression of "absolute knowledge."

Greatest elevation of man's *consciousness of
strength*, as that which creates superman.

If the universe had a goal, that goal would have
been reached by now. If any sort of unforeseen
final state existed, that state also would have been
reached. If it were capable of any halting or
stability of any "being," it would only have possessed this capability of becoming stable for one
instant in its development ; and again becoming
would have been at an end for ages, and with it all
thinking and all "spirit." The fact of "intellects"
being in a state of development proves that the uni-

verse can have no goal, no final state, and is incapable of being. But the old habit of thinking of some purpose in regard to all phenomena, and of thinking of a directing and creating deity in regard to the universe, is so powerful, that the thinker has to go to great pains in order to avoid thinking of the very aimlessness of the world as intended. The idea that the universe intentionally evades a goal, and even knows artificial means wherewith it prevents itself from falling into a circular movement, must occur to all those who would fain attribute to the universe the capacity of eternally regenerating itself — that is to say, they would fain impose upon a finite, definite force which is invariable in quantity, like the universe, the miraculous gift of renewing its forms and its conditions for all eternity. Although the universe is no longer a God, it must still be capable of the divine power of creating and transforming ; it must forbid itself to relapse into any one of its previous forms ; it must not only have the intention, but also the means, of avoiding any sort of repetition ; every second of its existence, even, it must control every single one of its movements, with the view of avoiding goals, final states, and repetitions — and all the other results of such an unpardonable and insane method of thought and desire. All this is nothing more than the old religious mode of thought and desire, which, in spite of all, longs to believe that in some way or other the universe resembles the old, beloved, infinite, and infinitely-creative God — that in some way or other "the old God still lives" — that longing of Spinoza's which is expressed in the words "*deus sive natura*" (what he really felt was "*natura sive deus*"). Which, then, is the proposition and belief in which the decisive change, the present preponderance of the scientific spirit over the religious and god-fancying spirit, is best formulated? Ought it not to be: the universe, as force, must not be thought of as unlimited, because it cannot be thought of in this way, — we forbid ourselves the concept infinite force, because it is incompatible with the idea of force? Whence it follows that the universe lacks the power of eternal renewal.

A certain emperor always bore the fleeting nature of all things in his mind, in order not to value them too seriously, and to be able to live quietly in their midst. Conversely, everything seems to me much too important for it to be so fleeting; I seek an eternity for everything: ought one to pour the most precious salves and wines into the sea? My consolation is that everything that has been is eternal: the sea will wash it up again.

And do ye know what "the universe" is to my mind? Shall I show it to you in my mirror? This universe is a monster of energy, without beginning or end; a fixed and brazen quantity of energy which grows neither bigger nor smaller, which does not consume itself, but only alters its face; as a whole its bulk is immutable, it is a household without either losses or gains, but likewise without increase and without sources of revenue, surrounded by nonentity as by a frontier. It is nothing vague or wasteful, it does not stretch into infinity; but is a definite quantum of energy located in limited space, and not in space which would be anywhere empty. It is rather energy everywhere, the play of forces and force-waves, at the same time one and many, agglomerating here and diminishing there, a sea of forces storming and raging in itself, for ever changing, for ever rolling back over incalculable ages to recurrence, with an ebb and flow of its forms, producing the most complicated things out of the most simple structures ; producing the most ardent, most savage, and most contradictory things out of the quietest, most rigid, and most frozen material, and then returning from multifariousness to uniformity, from the play of contradictions back into the delight of consonance, saying yea unto itself, even in this homogeneity of its courses and ages ; for ever blessing itself as something which recurs for all eternity, — a becoming which knows not satiety, or disgust, or weariness : — this, my Dionysian world of eternal self-creation, of eternal self-destruction, this mysterious world of twofold voluptuousness ; this, my "Beyond Good and Evil," without aim, unless there is an aim in the bliss of the circle, without will, unless a ring must by nature keep goodwill to itself, — would you have a name for my world ? A solution of all your riddles ? Do ye also want a light, ye most concealed, strongest and most undaunted men of the blackest midnight ? — *This world is the Will to Power — and nothing else !* And even ye yourselves are this will to power — and nothing besides !

* * *

IV

CONFESSIONS

My friends, we had a hard time as youths; we even suffered from youth itself as though it were a serious disease. This is owing to the age in which we were born — an age of enormous internal decay and disintegration which, with all its weakness and even with the best of its strength, is opposed to the spirit of youth. Disintegration — that is to say, uncertainty — is peculiar to this age: nothing stands on solid ground or on a sound faith. People live for the morrow, because the day-after-tomorrow is doubtful. All our road is slippery and dangerous, while the ice which still bears us has grown unconscionably thin: we all feel the mild and gruesome breath of the thaw-wind — soon, where we are walking, no one will any longer be able to stand!

The oftener a psychologist — a born, an unavoidable psychologist and soul-diviner — turns his attention to the more select cases and individuals, the greater becomes his danger of being suffocated by sympathy: he needs greater hardness and cheerfulness than any other man. For the corruption, the ruination of higher men, is in fact the rule: it is terrible to have such a rule always before our eyes. The manifold torments of the psychologist who has discovered this ruination, who discovers once, and then discovers almost repeatedly throughout all history, this universal inner "hopelessness" of higher men, this eternal "too late!" in every sense — may perhaps one day be the cause of his "going to the dogs" himself. In almost every psychologist we may see a tell-tale predilection in favour of intercourse with commonplace and well-ordered men : and this betrays how constantly he requires healing, that he needs a sort of flight and forgetfulness, away from what his insight and incisiveness — from what his "business" — has laid upon his conscience. A horror of his memory is typical of him. He is easily silenced by the judgment of others ; he hears with unmoved countenance how people honour, admire, love, and glorify, where he has opened his eyes and seen — or he even conceals his silence by expressly agreeing with some obvious opinion. Perhaps the paradox of his situation becomes so dreadful that, precisely where he has learnt *great sympathy*, together with *great contempt*, the educated have on their part learnt great reverence. And who knows but in all great instances, just this alone happened : that the multitude worshipped a God, and that the "God" was only a poor sacrificial animal ! *Success* has always been the greatest liar — and the "work" itself, the *deed*, is a success too ; the great statesman, the conqueror, the discoverer, are disguised in their creations until they can no longer be recognised ; the "work" of the artist, of the philosopher, only invents him who has created it, who is reputed to have created it ; the "great men," as they are reverenced, are poor little fictions composed afterwards ; in the world of historical values counterfeit coinage prevails.

The intellectual loathing and haughtiness of every man who has suffered deeply — the extent to which a man can suffer, almost determines the order of rank — the chilling uncertainty with which he is

thoroughly imbued and coloured, that by virtue of
his suffering he knows more than the shrewdest and
wisest can ever know, that he has been familiar
with, and "at home" in many distant terrible worlds
of which "you know nothing" ! — this silent intellectual haughtiness, this pride of the elect of knowledge, of the "initiated," of the almost sacrificed,
finds all forms of disguise necessary to protect itself
from contact with gushing and sympathising hands,
and in general from all that is not its equal in suffering. Profound suffering makes noble ; it separates. — One of the most refined forms of disguise is
Epicurism, along with a certain ostentatious bold-
ness of taste which takes suffering lightly, and puts
itself on the defensive against all that is sorrowful
and profound. There are "cheerful men" who
make use of good spirits, because they are misunderstood on account of them — they wish to be misunderstood. There are "scientific minds" who
make use of science, because it gives a cheerful appearance, and because love of science leads people
to conclude that a person is shallow — they wish to
mislead to a false conclusion. There are free in-
solent spirits which would fain conceal and deny
that they are at bottom broken, incurable hearts —
this is Hamlet's case : and then folly itself can be
the mask of an unfortunate and alas ! all too dead-
certain knowledge.

I have often asked myself whether I am not much
more deeply indebted to the hardest years of my
life than to any others. According to the voice
of my innermost nature, everything necessary, seen
from above and in the light of a superior economy,
is also useful in itself — not only should one bear

it, one should love it. . . *Amor fati*: this is the very core of my being. — And as to my prolonged illness, do I not owe much more to it than I owe to my health? To it I owe a *higher* kind of health, a sort of health which grows stronger under everything that does not actually kill it! — *To it, I owe even my philosophy.* . . Only great suffering is the ultimate emancipator of spirit; for it teaches one that vast suspiciousness which makes an X out of every U, a genuine and proper X, i.e., the antepenultimate letter: Only great suffering; that great suffering, under which we seem to be over a fire of greenwood, the suffering that takes its time — forces us philosophers to descend into our nethermost depths, and to let go of all trustfulness, all good-nature, all whittling-down, all mildness, all mediocrity, — on which things we had formerly staked our humanity. I doubt whether such suffering improves a man; but I know that it makes him *deeper.* . . Supposing we learn to set our pride, our scorn, our strength of will against it, and thus resemble the Indian who, however cruelly he may be tortured, considers himself revenged on his tormentor by the bitterness of his own tongue. Supposing we withdraw from pain into nonentity, into the deaf, dumb, and rigid sphere of self-surrender, self-forgetfulness, self-effacement: one is another person when one leaves these protracted and dangerous exercises in the art of self-mastery; one has one note of interrogation the more, and above all one has the will henceforward to ask more, deeper, sterner, harder, more wicked, and more silent questions, than anyone has ever asked on earth before. . . . Trust in life has vanished; life itself has become

a *problem.* — But let no one think that one has therefore become a spirit of gloom or a blind owl!
Even love of life is still possible, — but it is a different kind of love. . . It is the love for a woman
whom we doubt. . .

For, apart from the fact that I am a decadent, I
am also the reverse of such a creature. Among
other things my proof of this is, that I always
instinctively select the proper remedy when my
spiritual or bodily health is low ; whereas the decadent, as such, invariably chooses those remedies
which are bad for him. As a whole I was sound,
but in certain details I was a decadent. That energy with which I sentenced myself to absolute
solitude, and to a severance from all those conditions
in life to which I had grown accustomed ; my
discipline of myself, and my refusal to allow myself to be pampered, to be tended hand and foot,
and to be doctored — all this betrays the absolute
certainty of my instincts respecting what at that
time was most needful to me. I placed myself in
my own hands, I restored myself to health : the
first condition of success in such an undertaking,
as every physiologist will admit, is that at bottom a
man should be sound. An intrinsically morbid nature cannot become healthy. On the other hand,
to an intrinsically sound nature, illness may even
constitute a powerful stimulus to life, to a surplus
of life. It is in this light that I now regard the long
period of illness that I endured : it seemed as if I
had discovered life afresh, my own self included. I
tasted all good things and even trifles in a way in
which it was not easy for others to taste them —
out of my Will to Health and to Life I made my

philosophy. . . For this should be thoroughly understood; it was during those years in which my
vitality reached its lowest point that I ceased from
being a pessimist: the instinct of self-recovery for-
bade my holding to a philosophy of poverty and
desperation. Now, by what signs are Nature's
lucky strokes recognised among men? They are
recognised by the fact that any such lucky stroke
gladdens our senses; that he is carved from one
integral block, which is hard, sweet, and fragrant
as well. He enjoys that only which is good for
him; his pleasure, his desire, ceases when the limits
of that which is good for him are overstepped. He
divines remedies for injuries; he knows how to turn
serious accidents to his own advantage; that which
does not kill him makes him stronger. He instinctively gathers his material from all he sees,
hears, and experiences. He is a selective principle;
he rejects much. He is always in his own com-
pany, whether his intercourse be with books, with
men, or with natural scenery; he honours the
things he chooses, the things he acknowledges, the
things he trusts. He reacts slowly to all kinds of
stimuli, with that tardiness which long caution and
deliberate pride have bred in him — he tests the
approaching stimulus; he would not dream of meeting it half-way. He believes neither in "ill-luck"
nor "guilt"; he can digest himself and others; he
knows how to forget — he is strong enough to make
everything turn to his own advantage.

Lo then! I am the very reverse of a decadent,
for he whom I have just described is none other
than myself.

After the choice of nutrition, the choice of cli-

mate and locality, the third matter concerning
which one must not on any account make a blunder,
is the choice of the manner in which one *recuperates
one's strength*.   Here, again, according to the extent
to which a spirit is *sui generis*, the limits of that
which he can allow himself — in other words, the
limits of that which is beneficial to him — become
more and more confined.   As far as I in particular
am concerned, reading in general belongs to my
means of recuperation ; consequently it belongs to
that which rids me of myself, to that which enables
me to wander in strange sciences and strange souls
— to that, in fact, about which I am no longer in
earnest.   Indeed, it is while reading that I recover
from my earnestness.   During the time that I am
deeply absorbed in my work, no books are found
within my reach ; it would never occur to me to
allow anyone to speak or even to think in my presence.   For that is what reading would mean. . .
Has anyone ever actually noticed, that, during the
period of profound tension to which the state of
pregnancy condemns not only the mind, but also,
at bottom, the whole organism, accident and every
kind of external stimulus acts too acutely and strikes
too deep ?   Accident and external stimuli must, as
far as possible, be avoided : a sort of walling-of-
one's-self-in is one of the primary instinctive precau-
tions of spiritual pregnancy.   Shall I allow a strange
thought to steal secretly over the wall ?   For that
is what reading would mean. . . The periods of
work and fruitfulness are followed by periods of
recuperation : come hither, ye delightful, intellectual, intelligent books !   Shall I read German
books ? . . . I must go back six months to catch

myself with a book in my hand. I almost always take refuge in the same books: altogether their number is small; they are books which are precisely my proper fare. It is not perhaps in my nature to read much, and of all sorts: a library makes me ill. Neither is it my nature to love much or many kinds of things. Suspicion or even hostility towards new books is much more akin to my instinctive feeling than "toleration," *largeur de cœur*, and other forms of "neighbour-love." . . . It is to a small number of old French authors, that I always return again and again; I believe only in French culture, and regard everything else in Europe which calls itself "culture" as a misunderstanding. I do not even take the German kind into consideration. . . The few instances of higher culture with which I have met in Germany were all French in their origin. The most striking example of this was Madame Cosima Wagner, by far the most decisive voice in matters of taste that I have ever heard. If I do not read, but literally love Pascal, as the most instinctive sacrifice to Christianity, killing himself inch by inch, first bodily, then spiritually, according to the terrible consistency of this most appalling form of inhuman cruelty; if I have something of Montaigne's mischievousness in my soul, and — who knows? — perhaps also in my body; if my artist's taste endeavours to defend the names of Molière, Corneille, and Racine, and not without bitterness, against such a wild genius as Shakespeare — all this does not prevent me from regarding even the latter-day Frenchmen also as charming companions. I can think of absolutely no century in history, in

which a netful of more inquisitive and at the same
time more subtle psychologists could be drawn up
together than in the Paris of the present day. Let
me mention a few at random — for their number is
by no means small — Paul Bourget, Pierre Loti, Gyp,
Meilhac, Anatole France, Jules Lemaître ; or, to
point to one of strong race, a genuine Latin, of
whom I am particularly fond, Guy de Maupassant.
Between ourselves, I prefer this generation even to
its masters, all of whom were corrupted by German
philosophy (Taine, for instance, by Hegel, whom
he has to thank for his misunderstanding of great
men and great periods). Wherever Germany extends her sway, she ruins culture. It was the war
which first saved the spirit of France. . . Stendhal
is one of the happiest accidents of my life — for
everything that marks an epoch in it has been
brought to me by accident and never by means of a
recommendation. He is quite priceless, with his
psychologist's eye, quick at forestalling and anticipating ; with his grasp of facts, which is reminiscent
of the same art in the greatest of all masters of facts
(*ex ungue Napoleonem*) ; and, last but not least, as
an honest atheist — a specimen which is both rare
and difficult to discover in France — all honour to
Prosper Mérimée ! . . . Maybe that I am even en-
vious of Stendhal ? He robbed me of the best
atheistic joke, which I of all people could have
perpetrated : "God's only excuse is that He does not
exist." . . . I myself have said somewhere — What
has been the greatest objection to Life hitherto ? —
God. . .

*   *   *

It was *Heinrich Heine* who gave me the most perfect idea of what a lyrical poet could be. In vain do I search through all the kingdoms of antiquity or of modern times for anything to resemble his sweet and passionate music. He possessed that divine wickedness, without which perfection itself becomes unthinkable to me, — I estimate the value of men, of races, according to the extent to which they are unable to conceive of a god who has not a dash of the satyr in him. And with what mastery he wields his native tongue ! One day it will be said of Heine and me that we were by far the greatest artists of the German language that have ever existed, and that we left all the efforts that mere Germans made in this language an incalculable distance behind us.

Truth to tell, the number of ancient books that count for something in my life is but small ; and the most famous are not of that number. My sense of style, for the epigram as style, was awakened almost spontaneously upon my acquaintance with Sallust. I have not forgotten the astonishment of my respected teacher Corssen, when he was forced to give his worst Latin pupil the highest marks, — at one stroke I had learned all there was to learn. Condensed, severe, with as much substance as possible in the background, and with cold but roguish hostility towards all "beautiful words" and "beautiful feelings" — in these things I found my own particular bent. In my writings up to my "Zarathustra," there will be found a very earnest ambition to attain to the Roman style, to the "*aere perennius*" in style. — The same thing happened on my first acquaintance with Horace. Up to the present no poet has given me the same artistic raptures as those which from the first I received from an Horatian ode. In certain languages it would be absurd even to aspire to what is accomplished by this poet. This mosaic of words, in which every unit spreads its power to the left and to the right over the whole, by its sound, by its place in the sentence, and by its meaning, this minimum in the compass and number of the signs, and the maximum of energy in the signs which is thereby achieved — all this is Roman, and, if you will believe me, noble *par excellence*. By the side of this all the rest of poetry becomes something popular, — nothing more than senseless sentimental twaddle.

I am not indebted to the Greeks for anything like such strong impressions ; and, to speak frankly, they cannot be to us what the Romans are. One cannot learn from the Greeks — their style is too strange, it is also too fluid, to be imperative or to have the effect of a classic. Who would ever have learnt writing from a Greek ! Who would ever have learned it without the Romans ! . . .

At this point I can no longer evade a direct answer to the question, how one becomes what one is. And in giving it, I shall have to touch upon that masterpiece in the art of self-preservation, which is selfishness. . . Granting that one's life-task — the determination and the fate of one's life-task — greatly exceeds the average measure of deviations and aberrations, it prepares individual qualities and capacities, which one day will make themselves felt as indispensable to the whole of your task, — step by step it cultivates all the service-able faculties, before it ever whispers a word concerning the dominant task, the "goal," the "object," and the "meaning" of it all. Looked at from this standpoint my life is simply amazing. For the task of transvaluing values, more capacities were needful perhaps than could well be found side by side in one individual ; and above all, antagonistic capacities which had to be free from the mutual strife and destruction which they involve. An order of rank among capacities ; distance ; the art of separating without creating hostility ; to refrain from confounding things ; to keep from reconciling things ; to possess enormous multifariousness and yet to be the reverse of chaos — all this was the first condition, the long secret work, and the artistic mastery of my instinct. Its superior guardianship manifested itself with such exceeding strength, that not once did I ever dream of what was growing within me — until suddenly all my capacities were ripe, and one day burst forth in all the perfection of their highest bloom. I cannot remember ever having exerted myself, I can point to no trace of struggle in my life ; I am the reverse of a heroic nature. To "will" something, to "strive" after something, to have an "aim" or a "desire" in my mind — I know none of these things from experience. Even at this moment I look out upon my future — a *broad* future ! — as upon a calm sea : no sigh of longing makes a ripple on its surface. I have not the slightest wish that anything should be otherwise than it is : I myself would not be otherwise. . . But in this matter I have always been the same. I have never had a desire. A man who, after his four-and-fortieth year, can say that he has never bothered himself about *honours, women,* or *money* ! — not that they did not come his way. . . It was thus that I became one day a University Professor — I had never had the remotest idea of such a thing ; for I was scarcely four-and-twenty years of age. In the same way, two years previously, I had one day become a philologist, in the sense that my first philological work, my start in every way, was expressly obtained by my master Ritschl for publication in his Rheinisches Museum.

You may be wondering why I should actually have related all these trivial and, according to traditional accounts, insignificant details to you ; such action can but tell against me, more particularly if I am fated to figure in great causes. To this I reply that these trivial matters — diet, locality, climate, and one's mode of recreation, the whole casuistry of self-love — are inconceivably more important than all that which has hitherto been held in high esteem. It is precisely in this quarter that we must begin to learn afresh. All those things which mankind has valued with such earnestness heretofore are not even real ; they are mere creations of fancy, or, more strictly speaking, *lies* born of the evil instincts of diseased and, in the deepest sense, noxious natures — all the concepts, "God," "soul," "virtue," "sin," "Beyond," "truth," "eternal life." . . . But the greatness of human nature, its "divinity," was sought for in them. . . All questions of politics, of social order, of education, have been falsified, root and branch, owing to the fact that the most noxious men have been taken for great men, and that people were taught to despise the small things, or rather the *fundamental* things, of life. If I now choose to compare myself with those creatures who have hitherto been honoured as the first among men, the difference becomes obvious. I do not reckon the so-called "first" men even as human beings — for me they are the excrements of mankind, the products of disease and of the instinct of revenge : they are so many monsters laden with rottenness, so many hopeless incurables, who avenge themselves on life. . . I wish to be the opposite of these people : it is my privilege to have the very sharpest discernment for every sign of healthy instincts. There is no such thing as a morbid trait in me ; even in times of serious illness I have never grown morbid, and you might seek in vain for a trace of fanaticism in my nature. No one can point to any moment of my life in which I have assumed either an arrogant or a pathetic attitude. Pathetic attitudes are not in keeping with greatness ; he who needs attitudes is false. . . Beware of all picturesque men ! Life was easy — in fact easiest — to me, in those periods when it exacted the heaviest duties from me. Whoever could have seen me during the seventy days of this autumn, when, without interruption, I did a host of things of the highest rank — things that no man can do nowadays — with a sense of responsibility for all the ages yet to come, would have noticed no sign of tension in my condition, but rather a state of overflowing freshness and good cheer. Never have I eaten with more pleasant sensations, never has my sleep been better. I know of no other manner of dealing with great tasks, than as *play* : this, as a sign of greatness, is an essential prerequisite. The slightest constraint, a sombre mien, any hard accent in the voice — all these things are objections to a man, but how much more to his work ! . . . One must not have nerves. . . Even to *suffer* from solitude is an objection — the only thing I have always suffered from is "multitude." At an absurdly tender age, in fact when I was seven years old, I already knew that no human speech would ever reach me : did anyone ever see me sad on that account ? At present I still possess the same affability towards everybody, I am even full of consideration for the lowest : in all this there is not an atom of haughtiness or of secret contempt. He whom I despise soon guesses that he is despised by me : the very fact of my existence is enough to rouse indignation in all those who have polluted blood in their veins. My formula for greatness in man is *amor fati* : the fact that a man wishes nothing to be different, either in front of him or behind him, or for all eternity. Not only must the necessary be borne, and on no account concealed, — all idealism is falsehood in the face of necessity, — but it must also be *loved* . . .

I *know* my destiny. There will come a day when my name will recall the memory of something formidable — a crisis the like of which has never been known on earth, the memory of the most profound clash of consciences, and the passing of a sentence upon all that which theretofore had been believed, exacted, and hallowed. I am not a man, I am dynamite. And with it all there is nought of the founder of a religion in me. Religions are matters for the mob ; after coming in contact with a religious man, I always feel that I must wash my hands. . . I require no "believers,"

it is my opinion that I am too full of malice to believe even in myself ; I never address myself to
masses.   I am horribly frightened that one day I
shall be pronounced "holy.".   You will understand
why I publish this book beforehand — it is to prevent people from wronging me.   I refuse to be a
saint ; I would rather be a clown.   Maybe I am a
clown.   And I am notwithstanding, or rather not
*not*withstanding, the mouthpiece of truth ; for
nothing more blown-out with falsehood has ever
existed, than a saint.   But my truth is terrible :
for hitherto lies have been called truth.   *The
Transvaluation of all Values*, this is my formula
for mankind's greatest step towards coming to its
senses — a step which in me became flesh and genius.
My destiny ordained that I should be the first de-
cent human being, and that I should feel myself opposed to the falsehood of millenniums.   I was the
first to discover truth, and for the simple reason
that I was the first who became conscious of falsehood as falsehood — that is to say, I smelt it as such.
My genius resides in my nostrils.   I contradict as
no one has contradicted hitherto, and am nevertheless the reverse of a negative spirit.   I am the
harbinger of joy, the like of which has never existed before ; I have discovered tasks of such lofty
greatness that, until my time, no one had any idea
of such things.   Mankind can begin to have fresh
hopes, only now that I have lived.   Thus, I am
necessarily a man of Fate.   For when Truth enters
the lists against the falsehood of ages, shocks are
bound to ensue, and a spell of earthquakes, followed
by the transposition of hills and valleys, such as the
world has never yet imagined even in its dreams.

The concept "politics" then becomes elevated entirely to the sphere of spiritual warfare. All the mighty realms of the ancient order of society are blown into space — for they are all based on falsehood : there will be wars, the like of which have never been seen on earth before. Only from my time and after me will politics on a large scale exist on earth.

* * *

ONCE MORE

UNTO ALL ETERNITY

O man ! Take heed !
What saith deep midnight's voice indeed ?
"I slept my sleep — ,
"From deepest dream I've woke, and plead : —
"The world is deep,
"And deeper than the day could read.
"Deep is its woe — ,
"Joy — deeper still than grief can be :
"Woe saith : Hence ! Go !
"But joys all want eternity — ,
" — Want deep, profound eternity !"